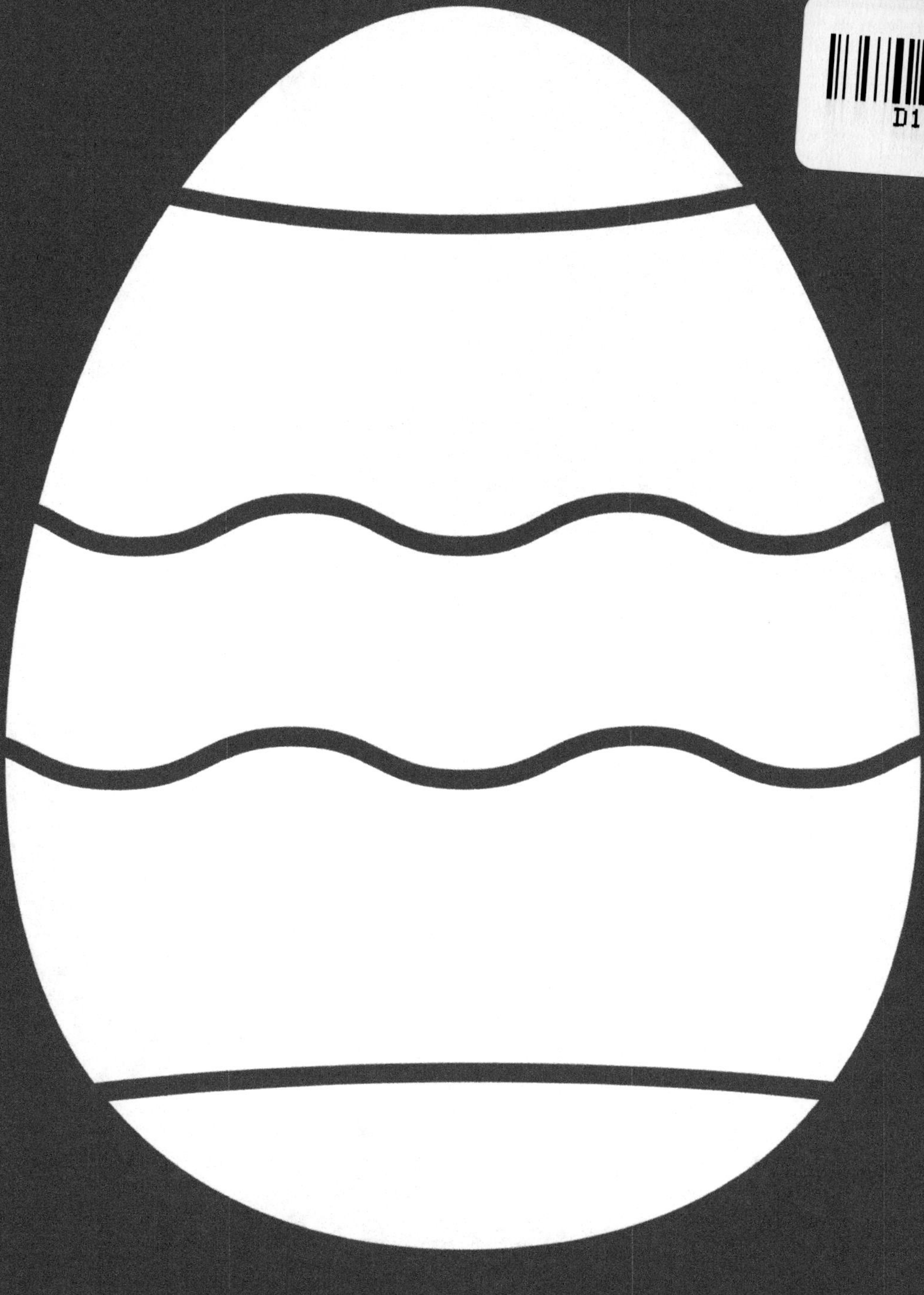

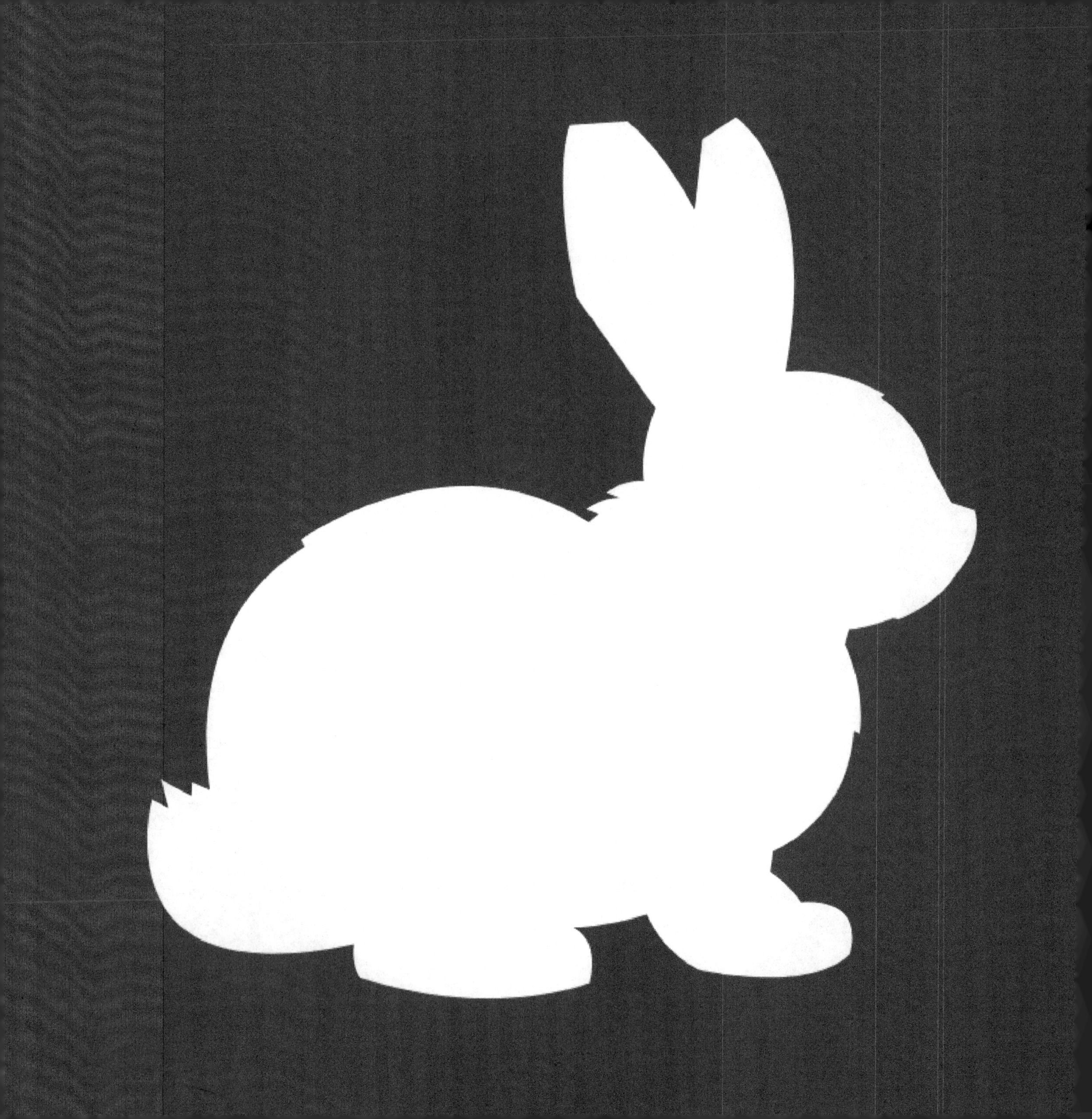

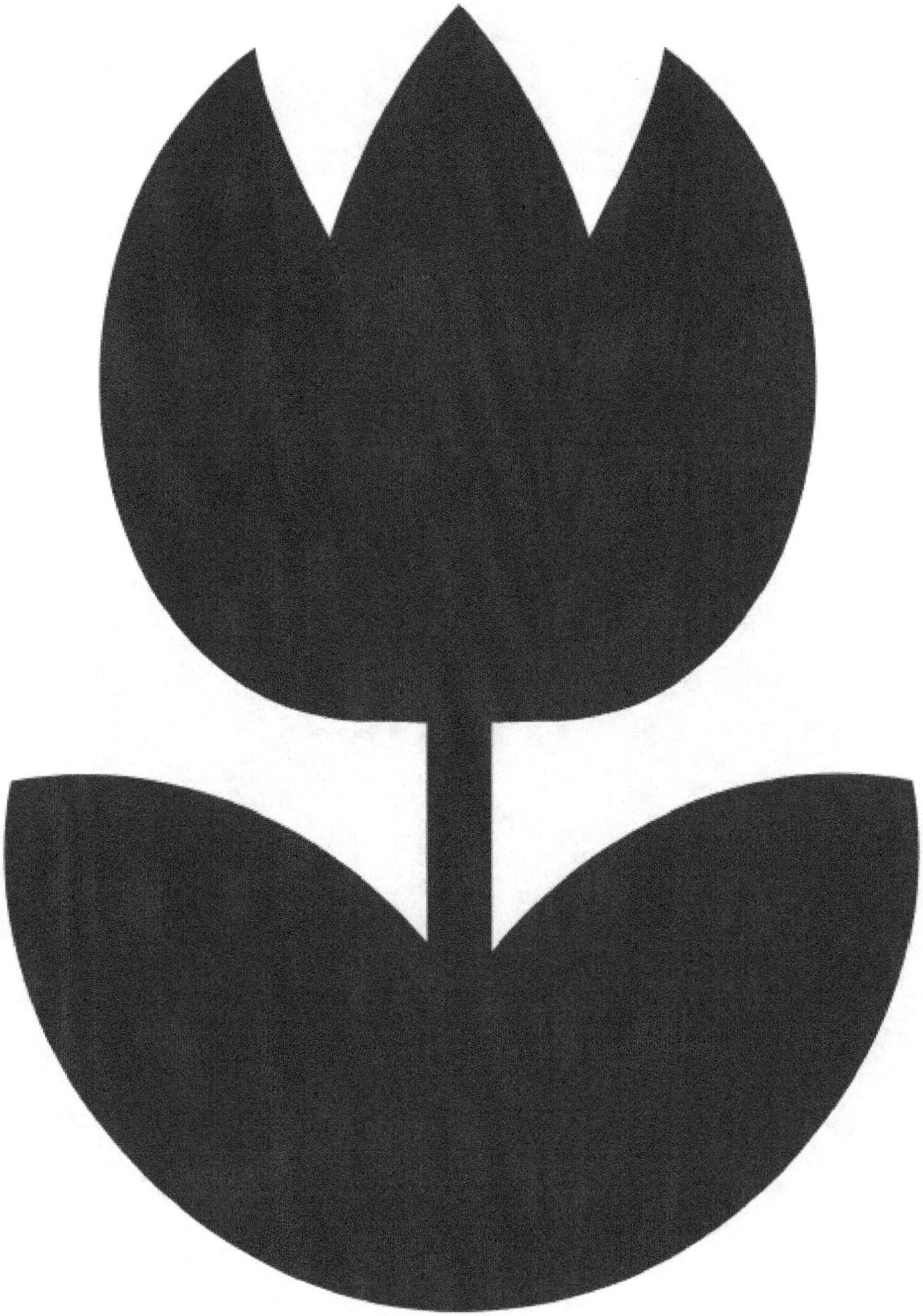

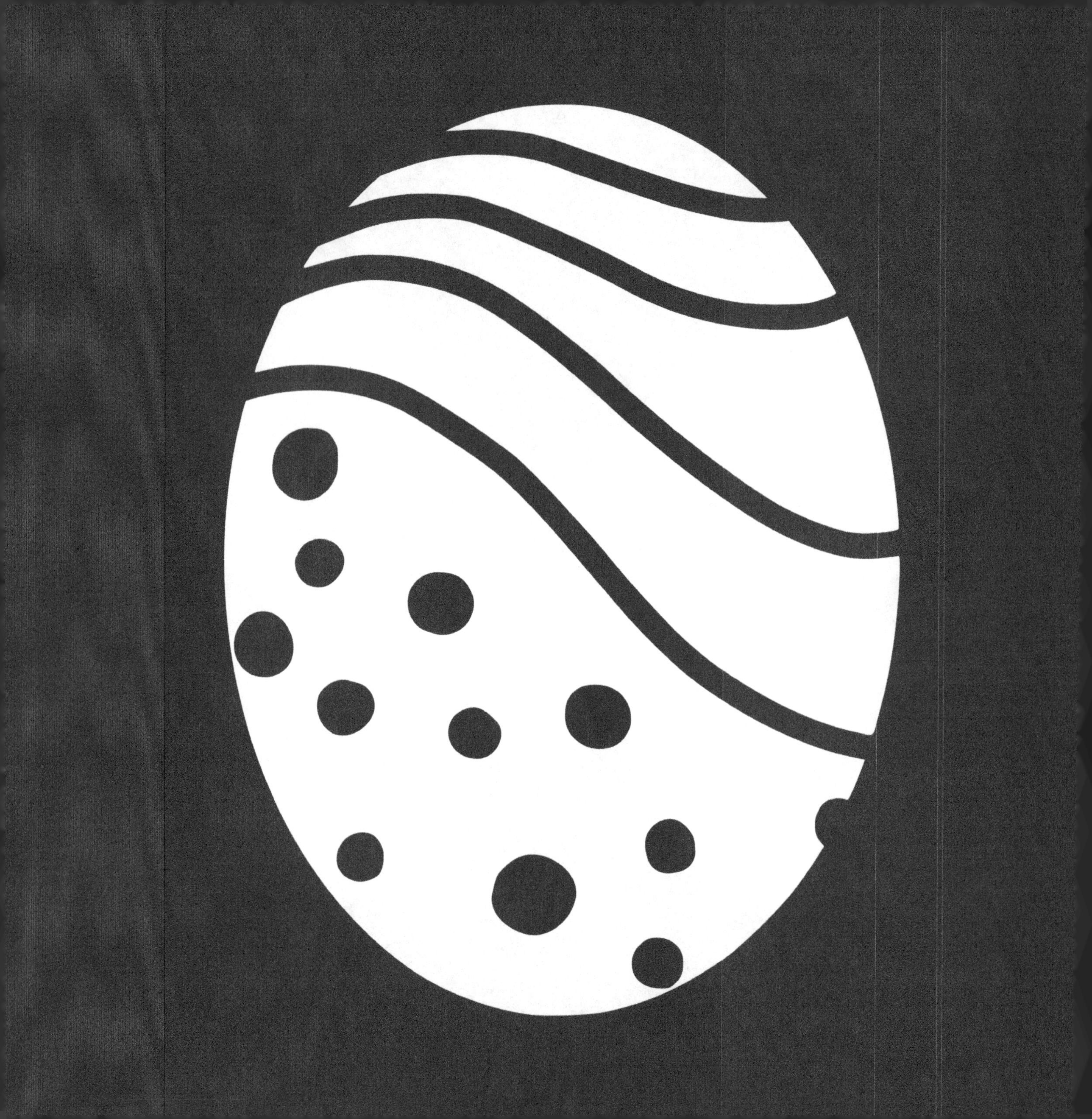

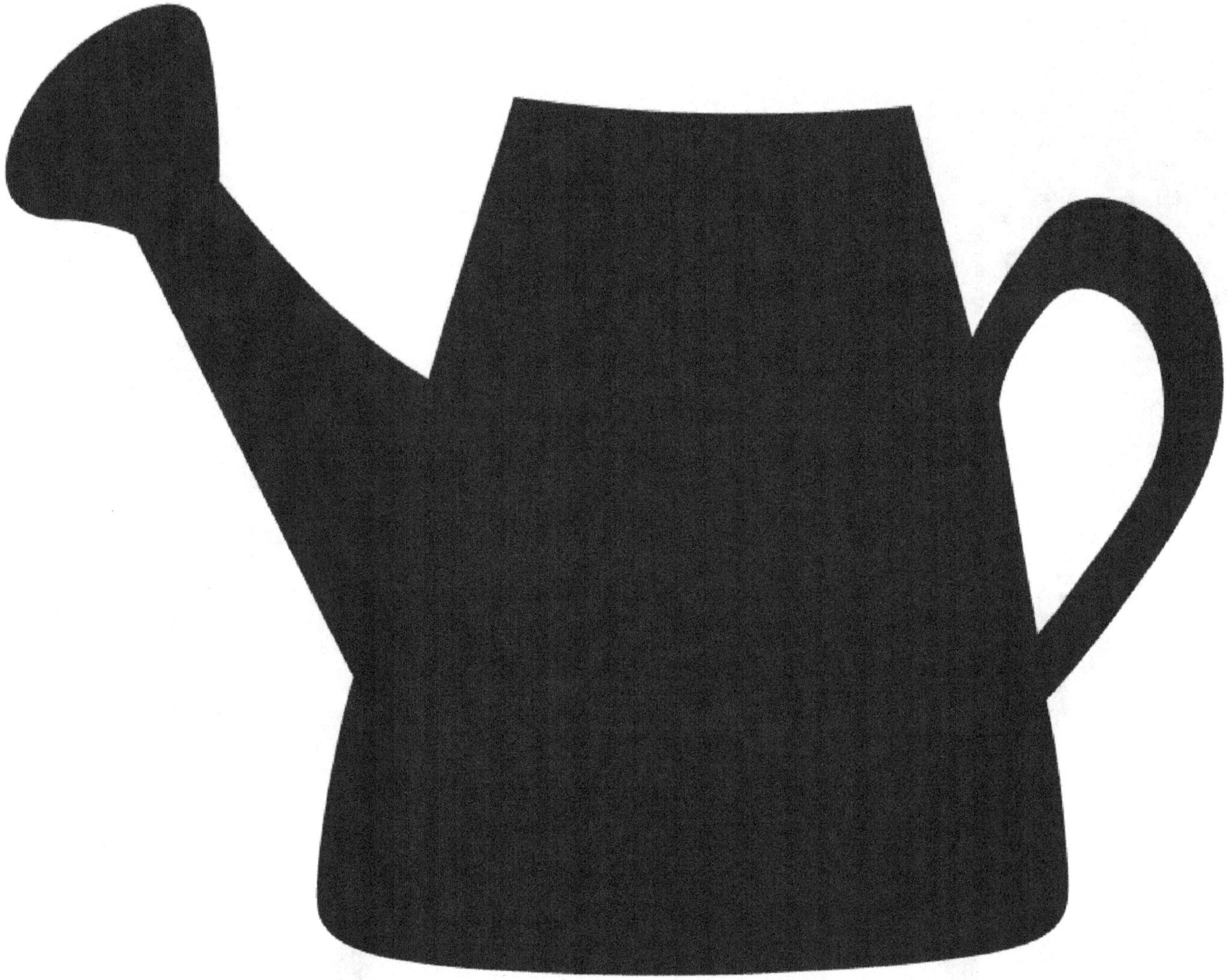

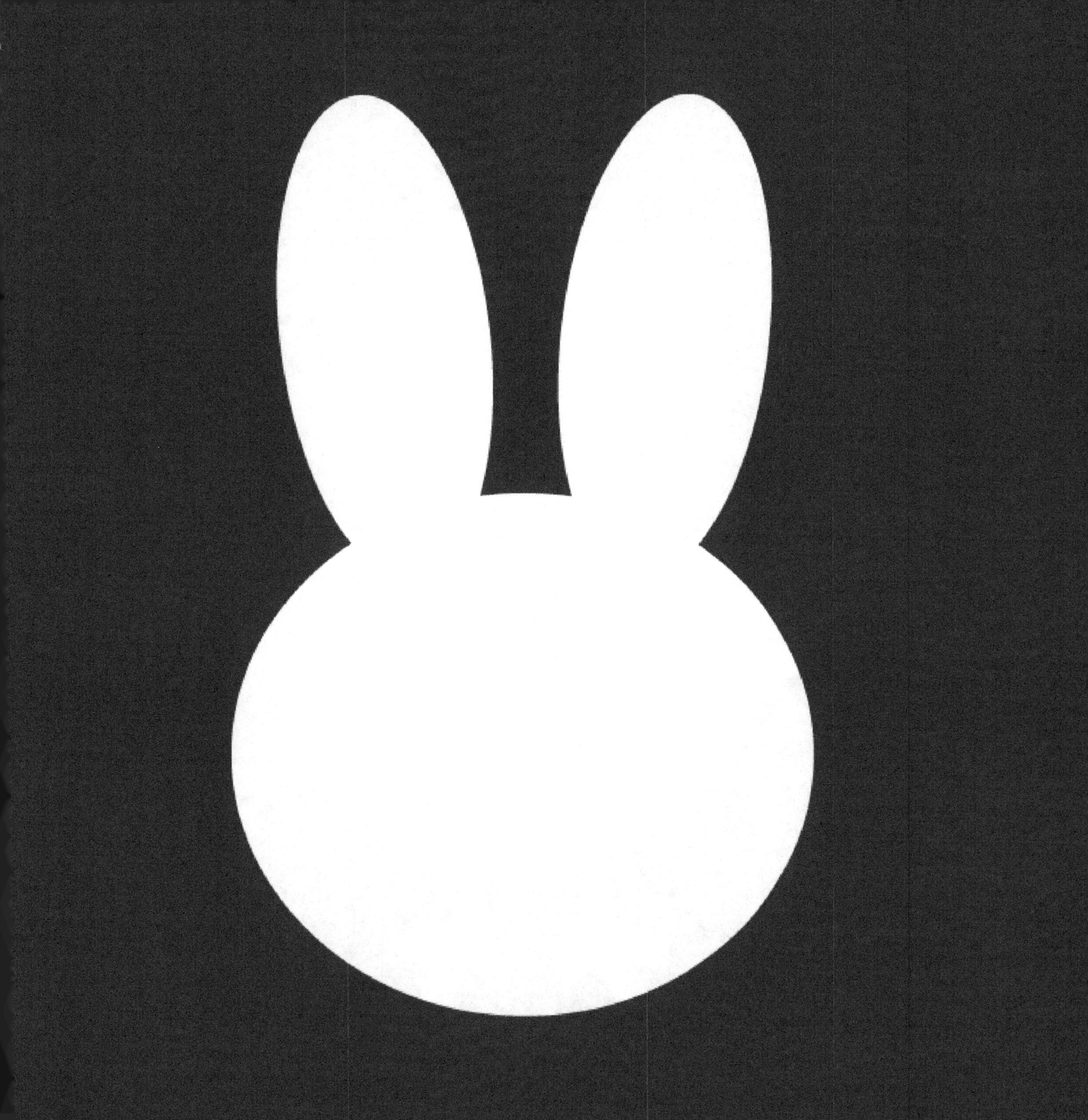

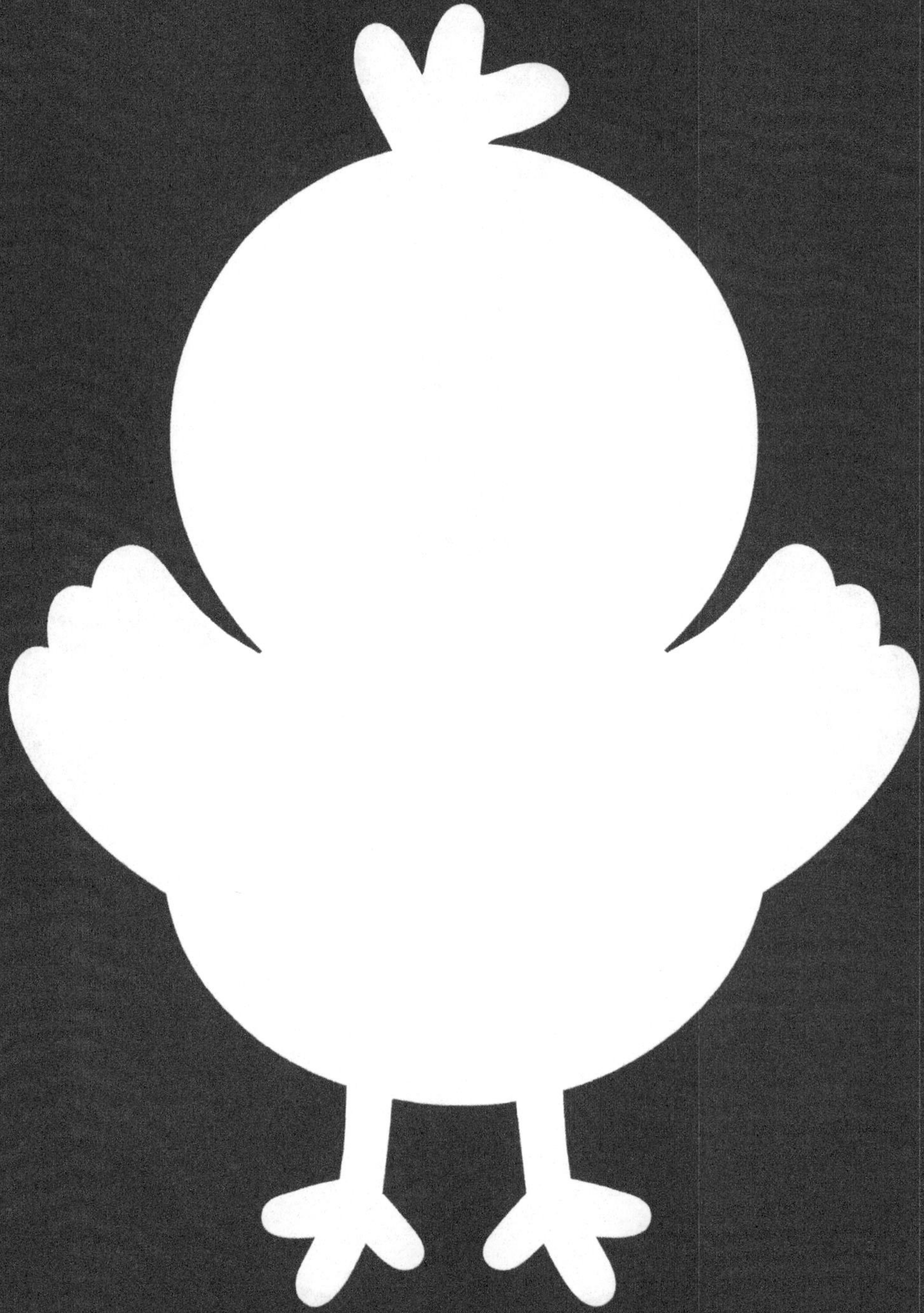

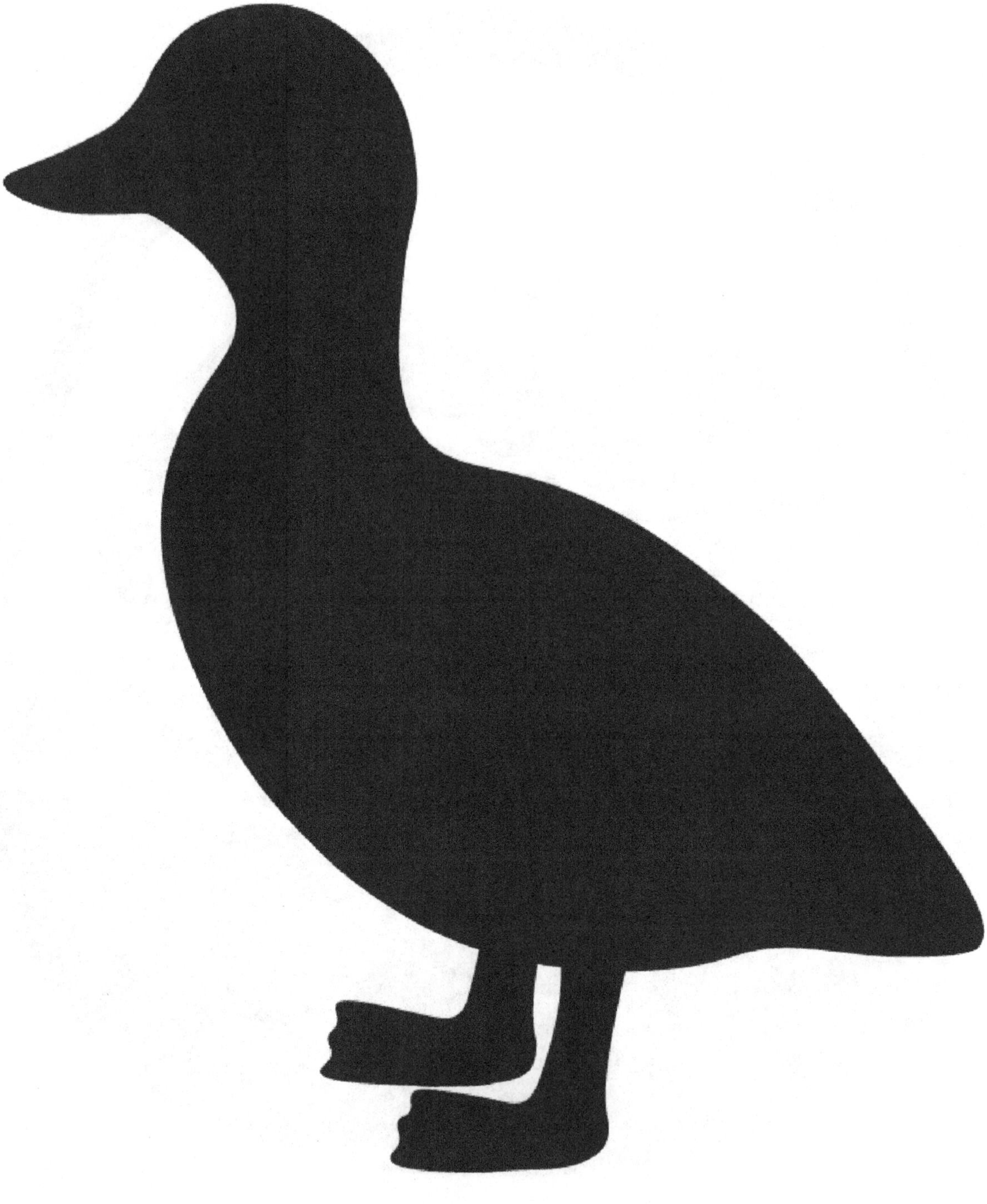

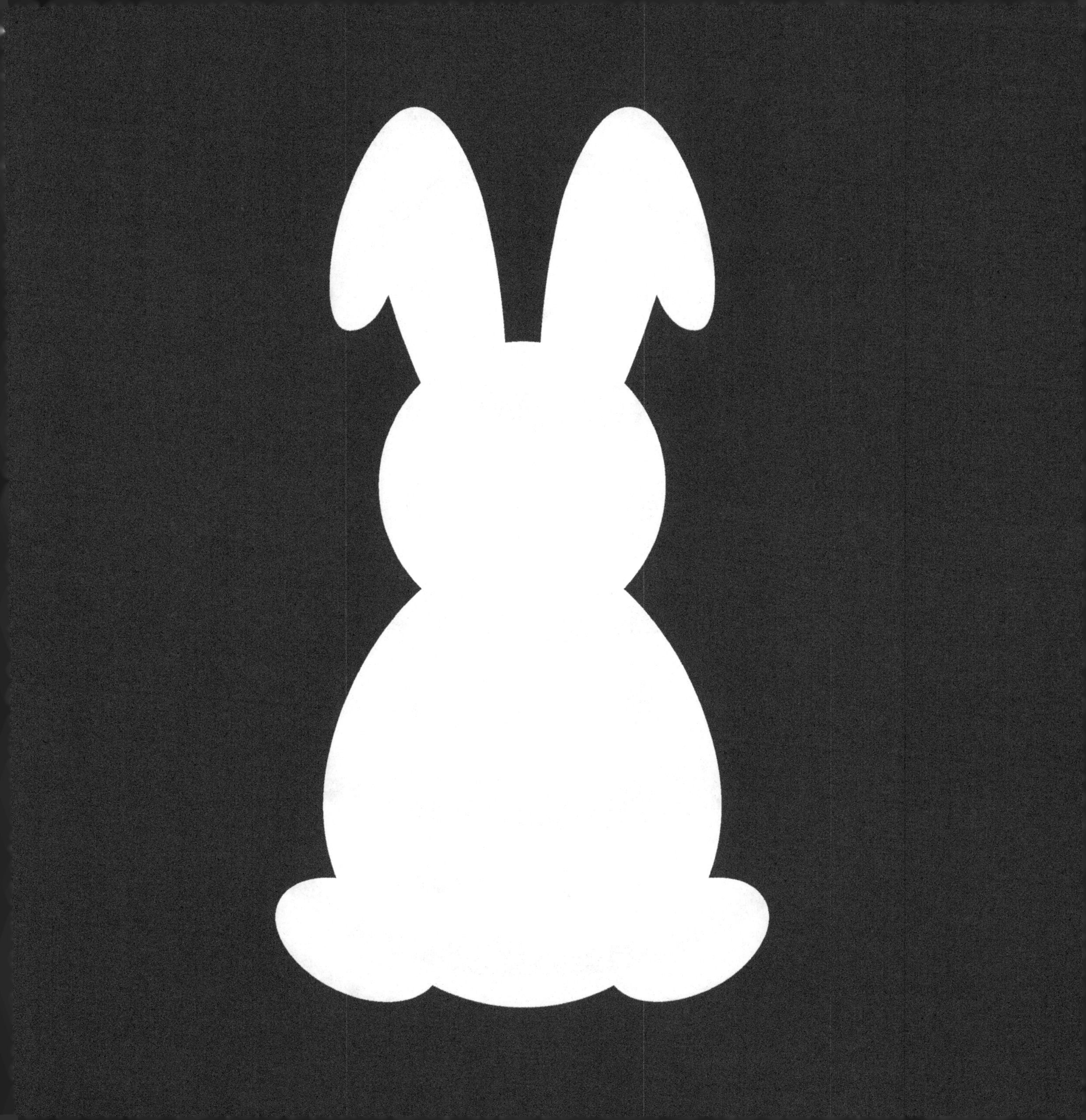

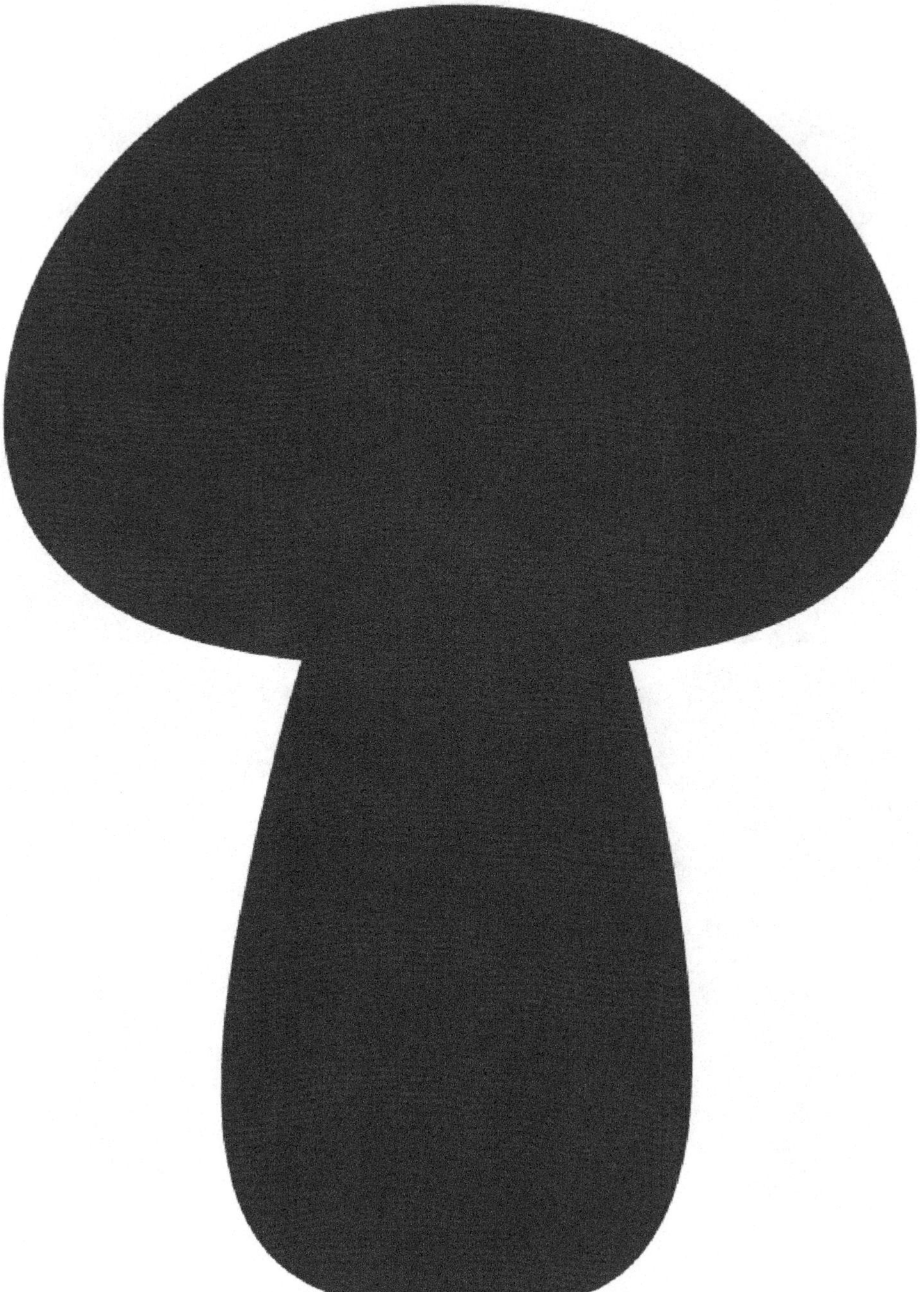

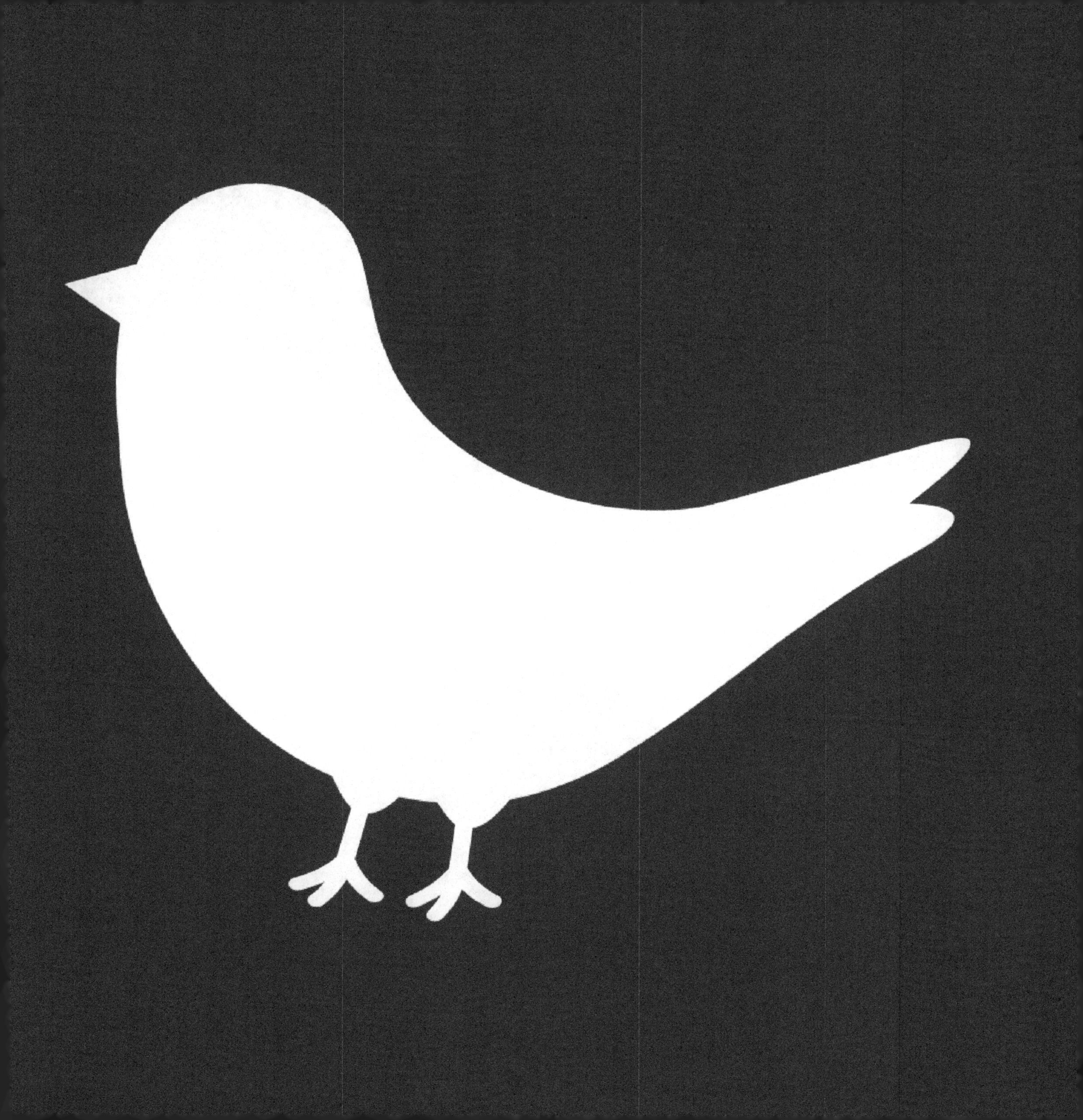

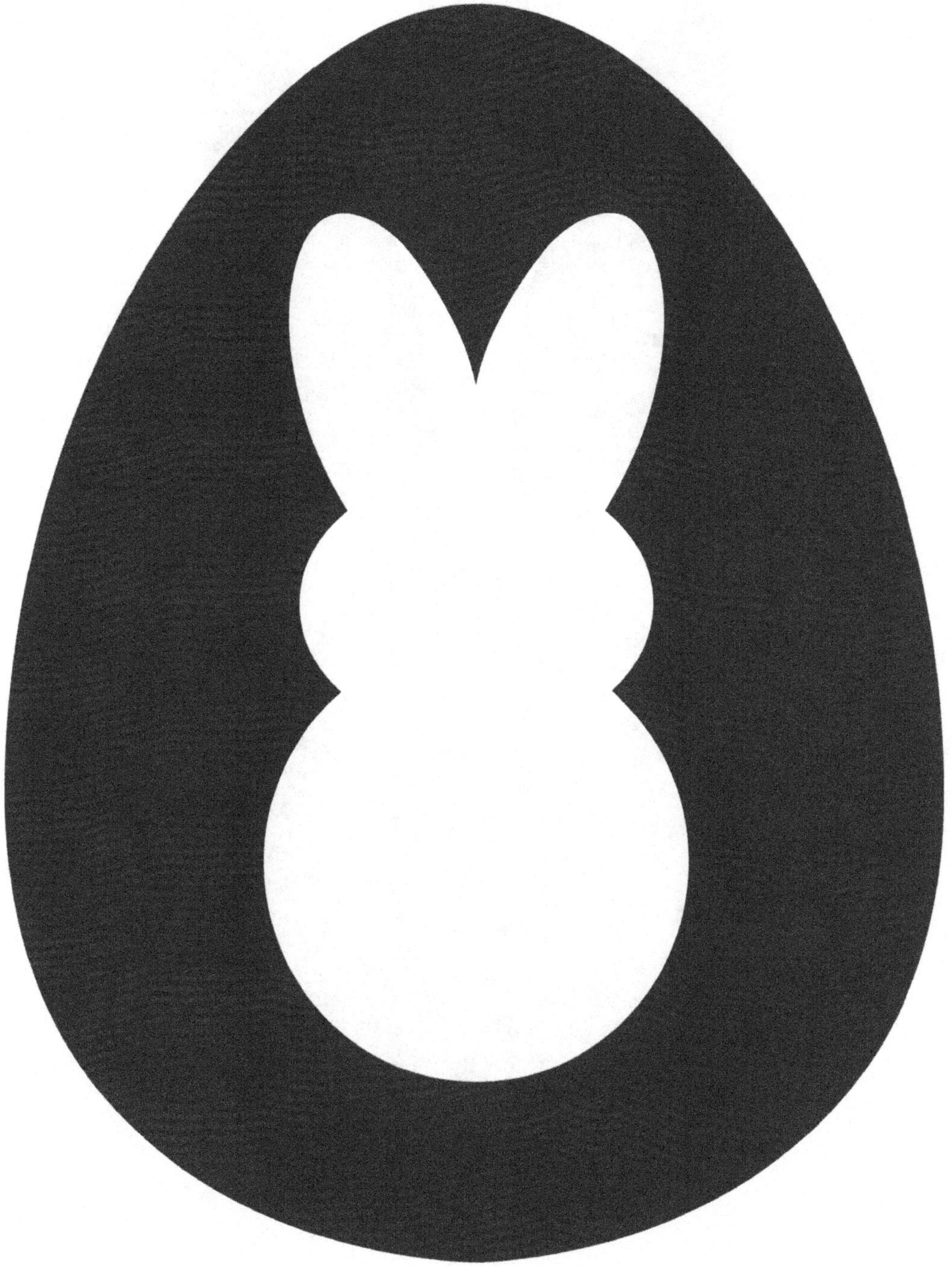

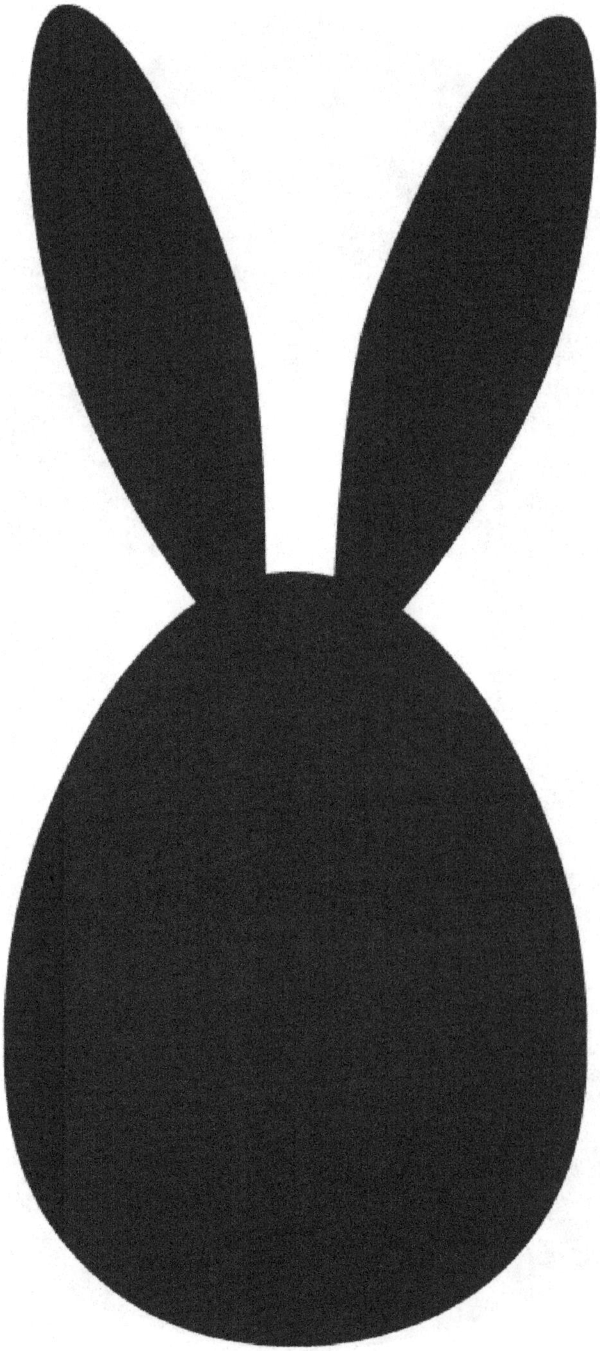

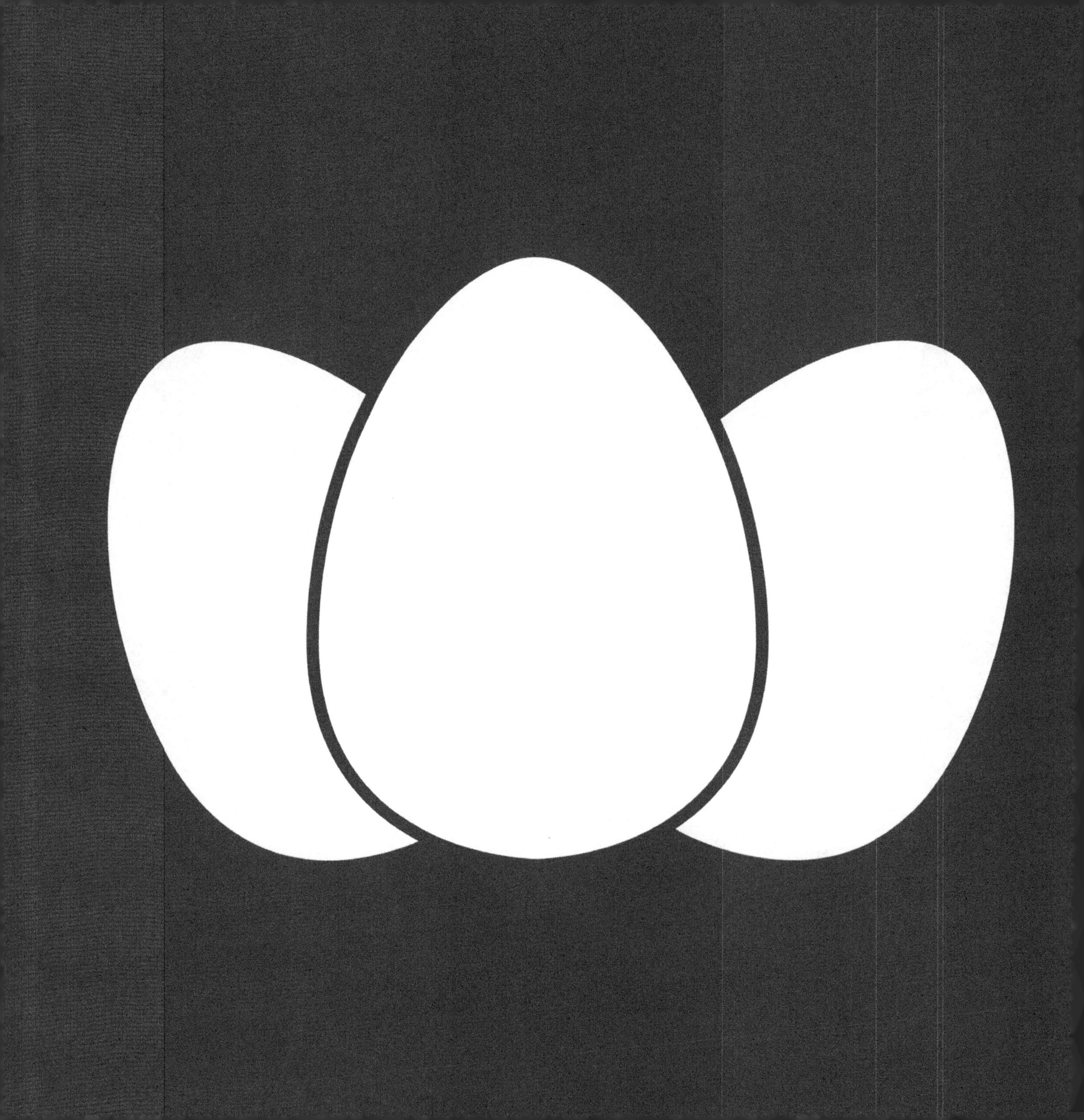

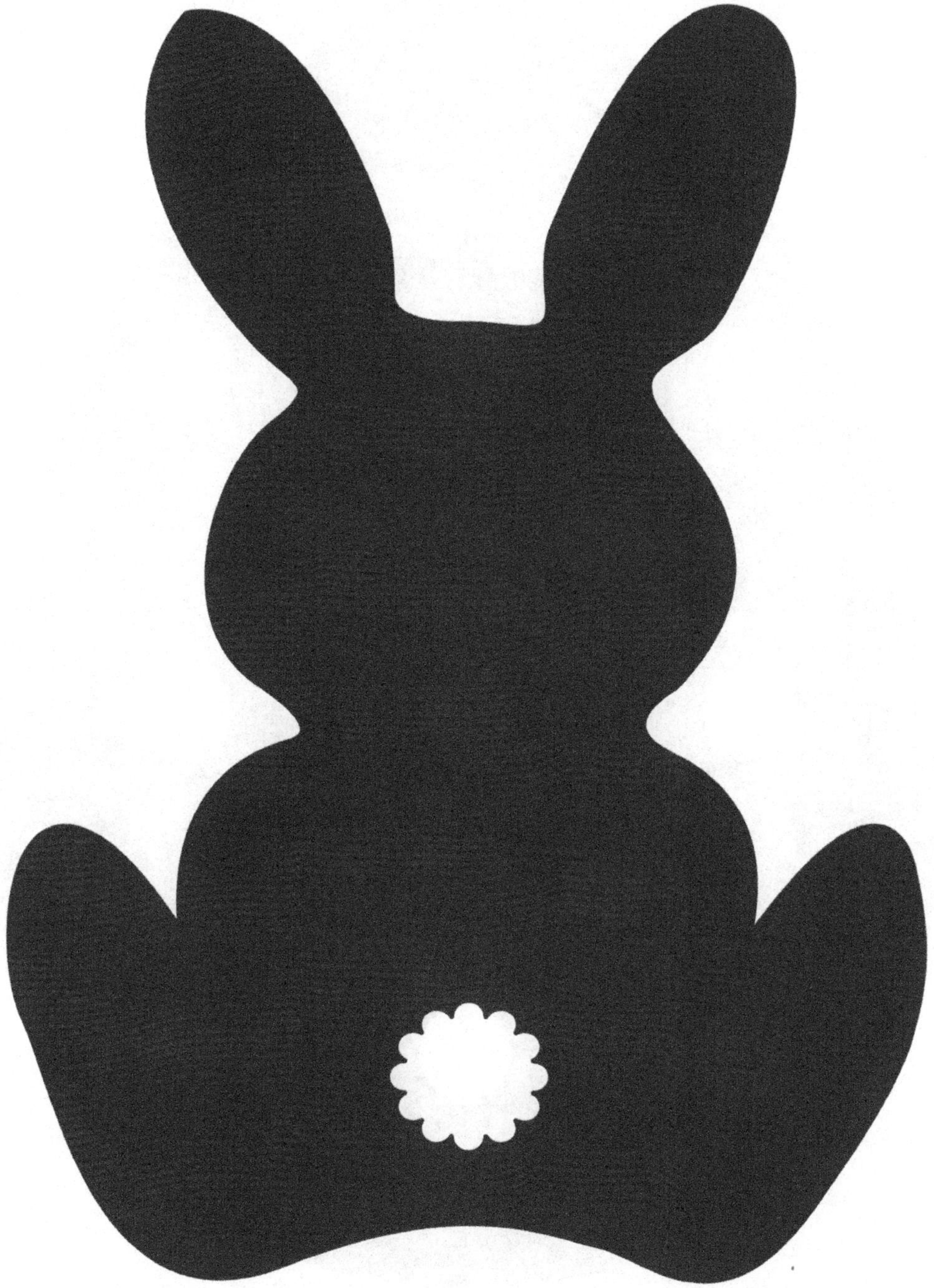

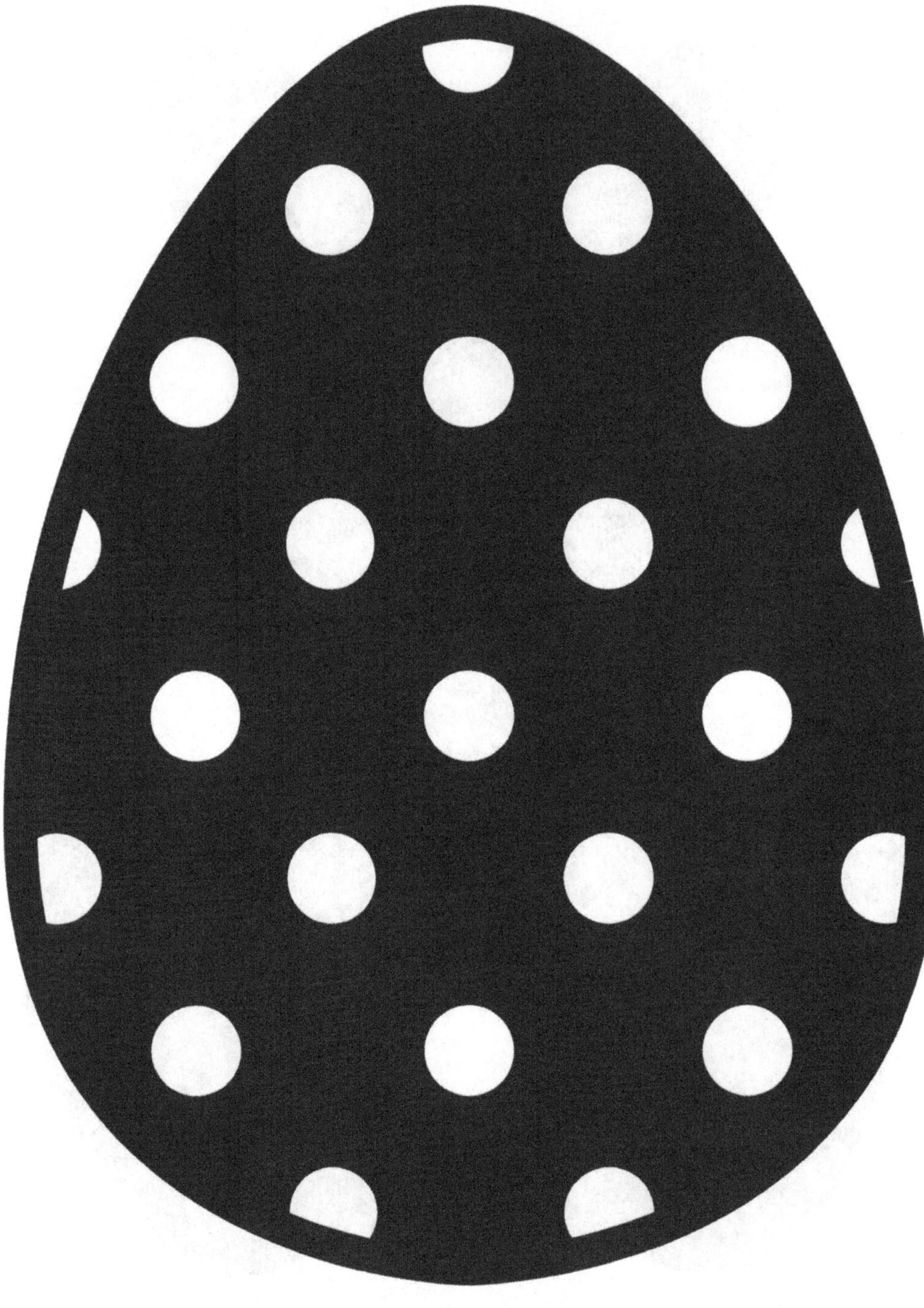

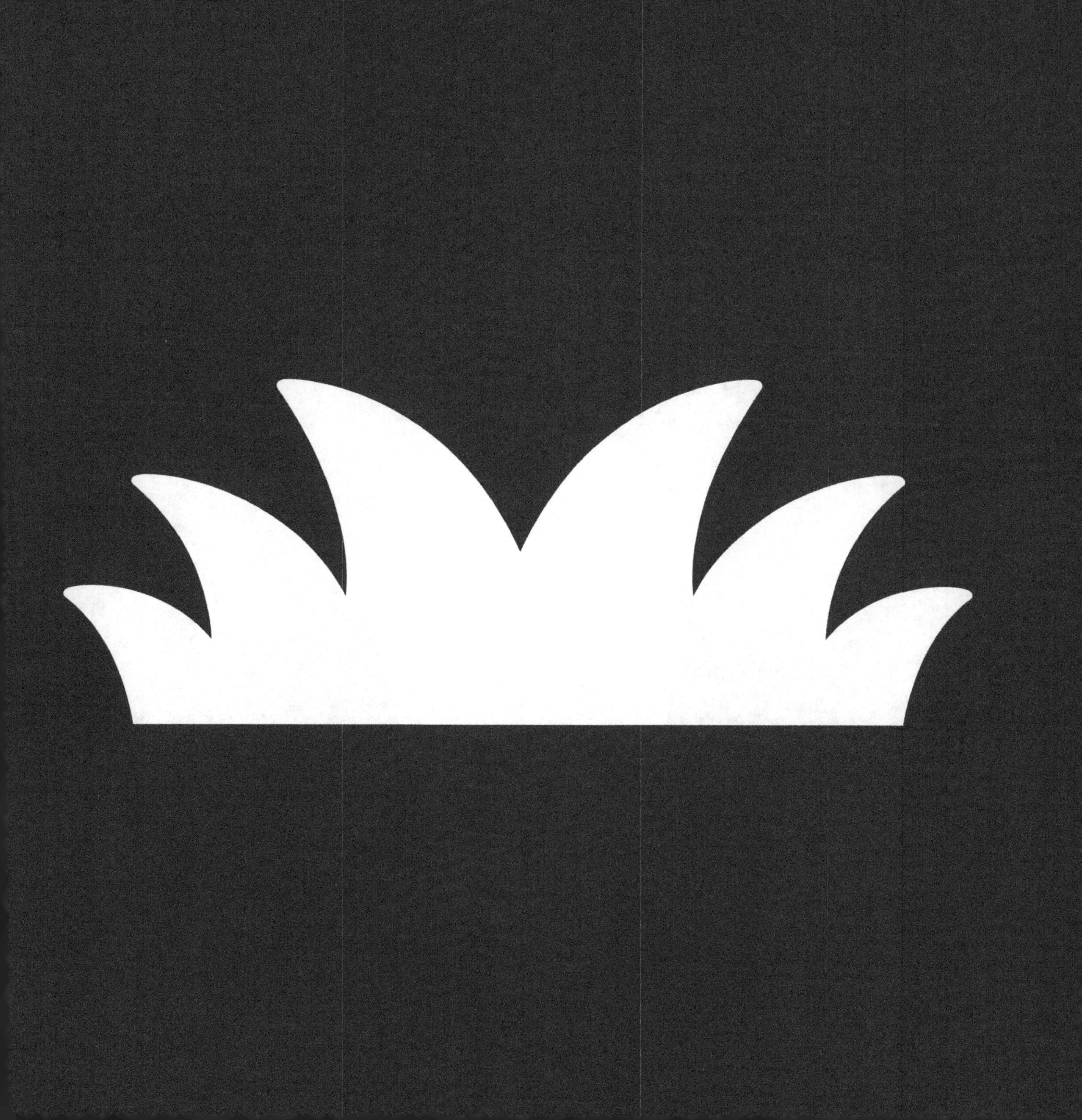

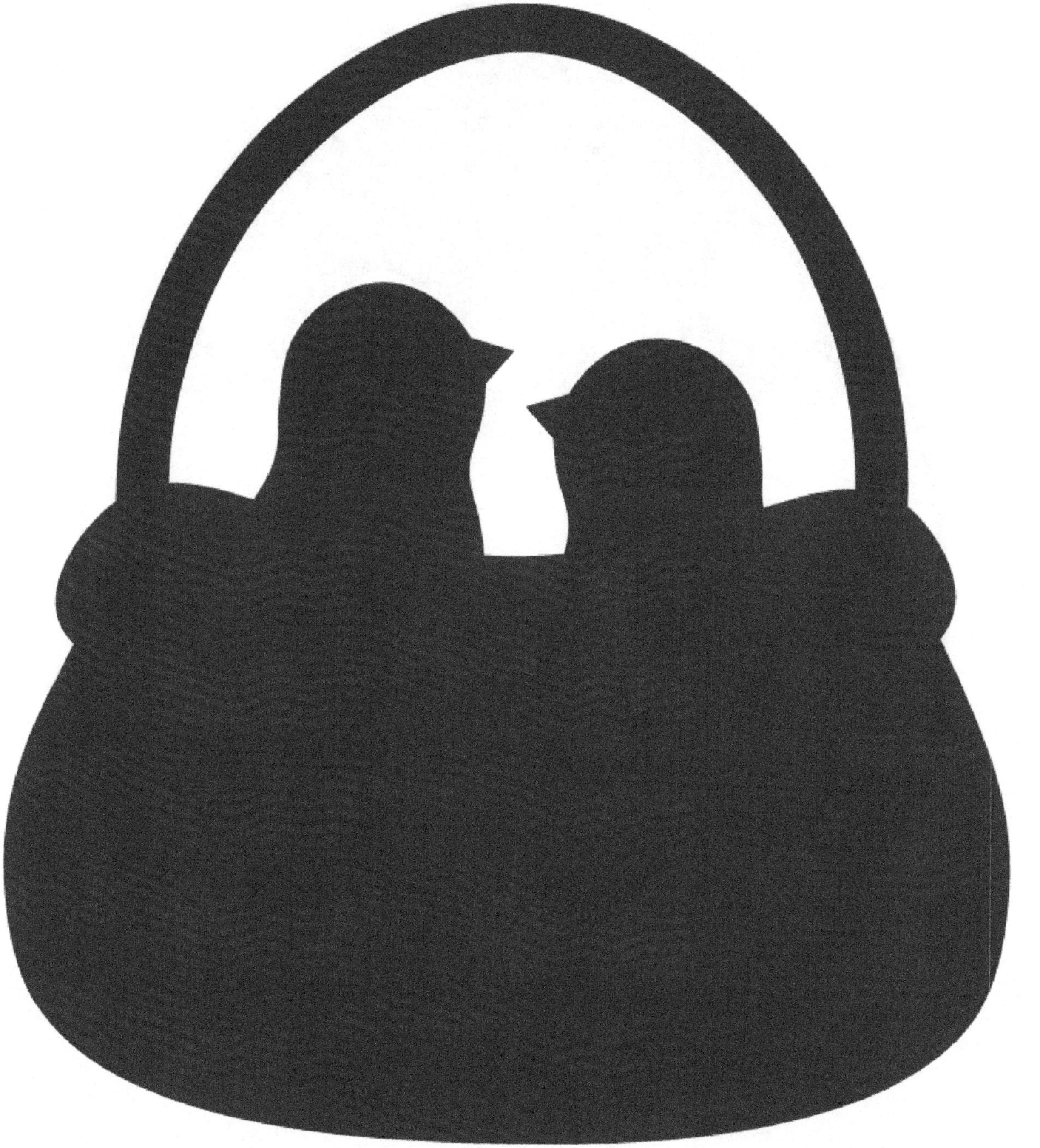

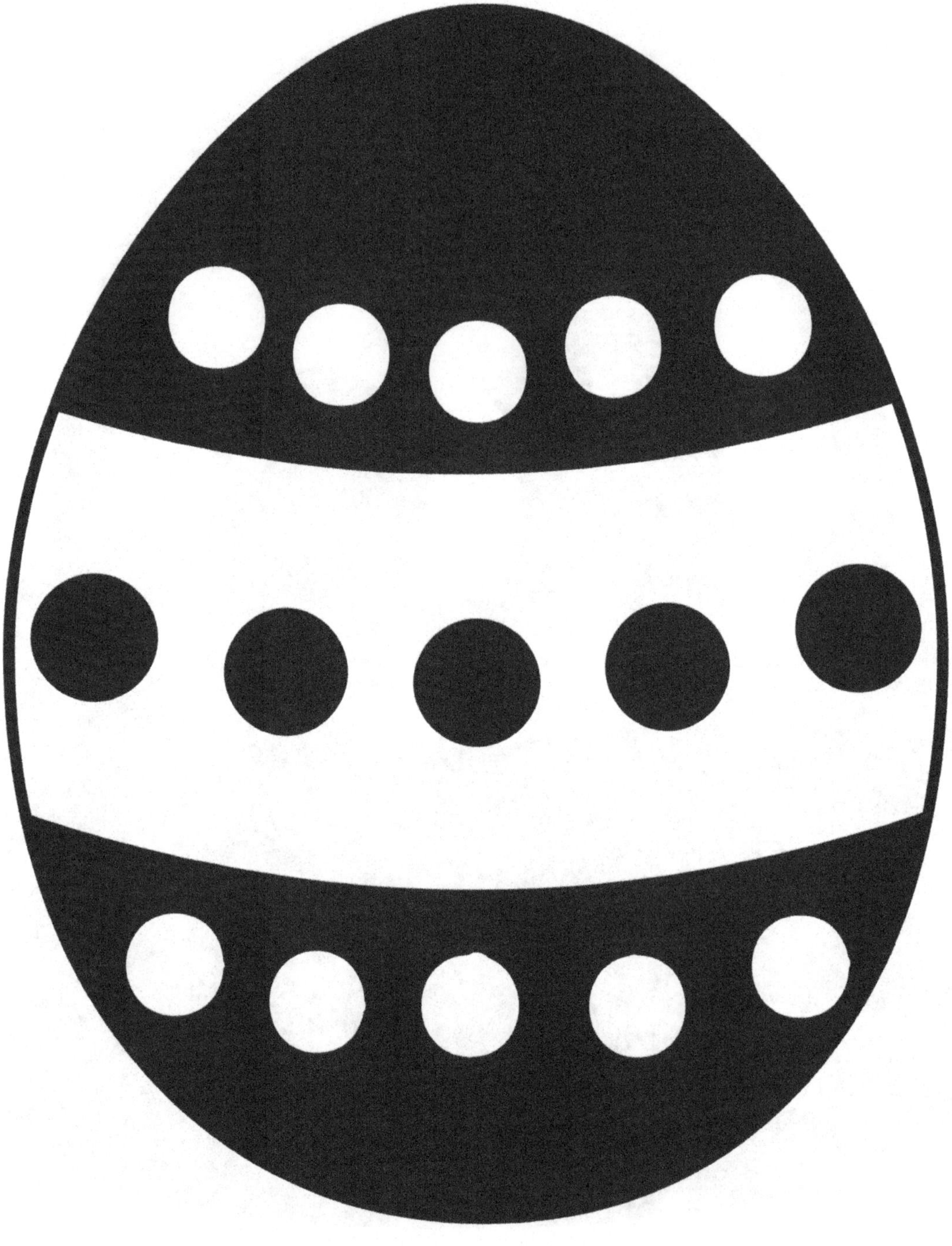

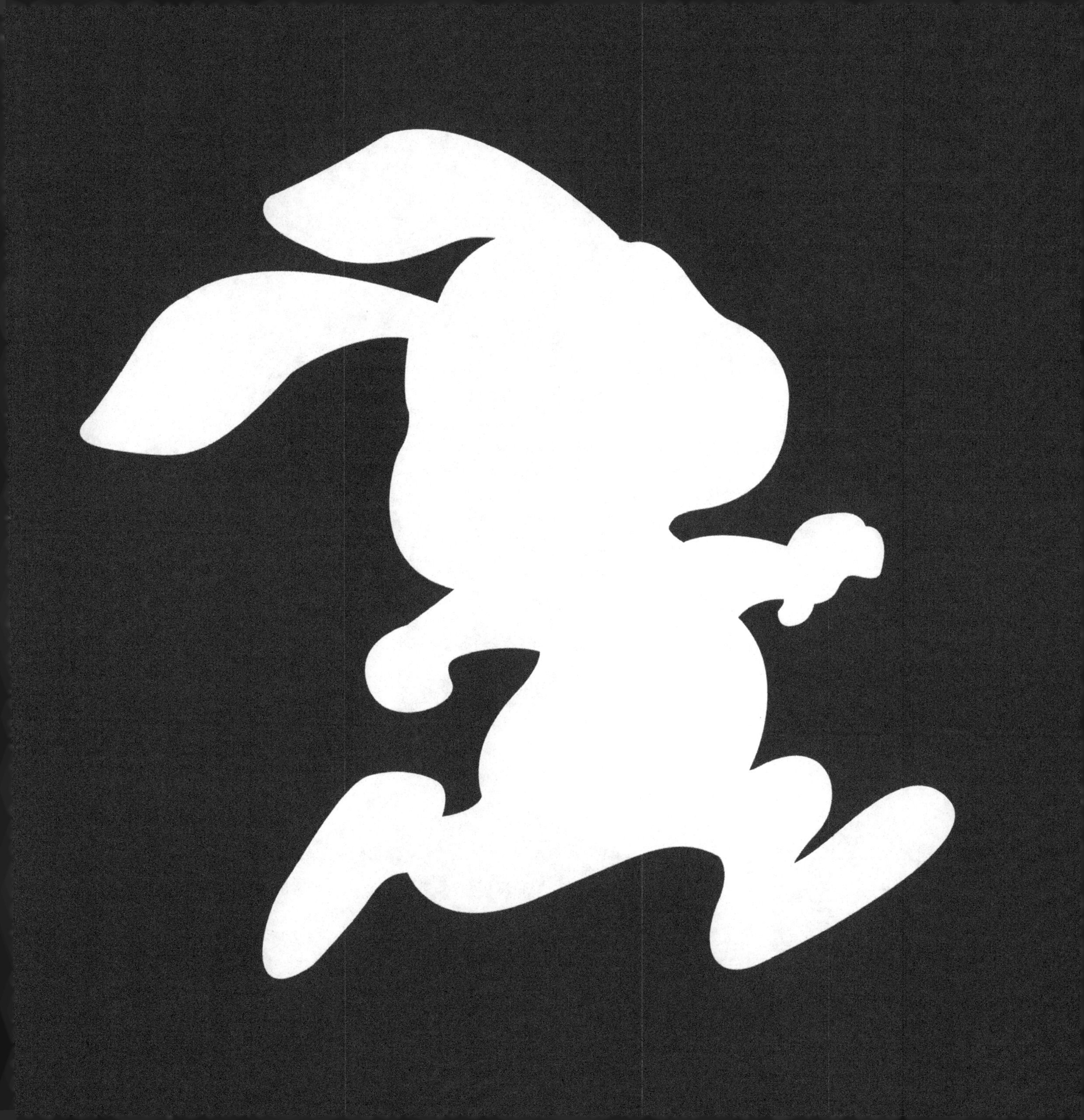

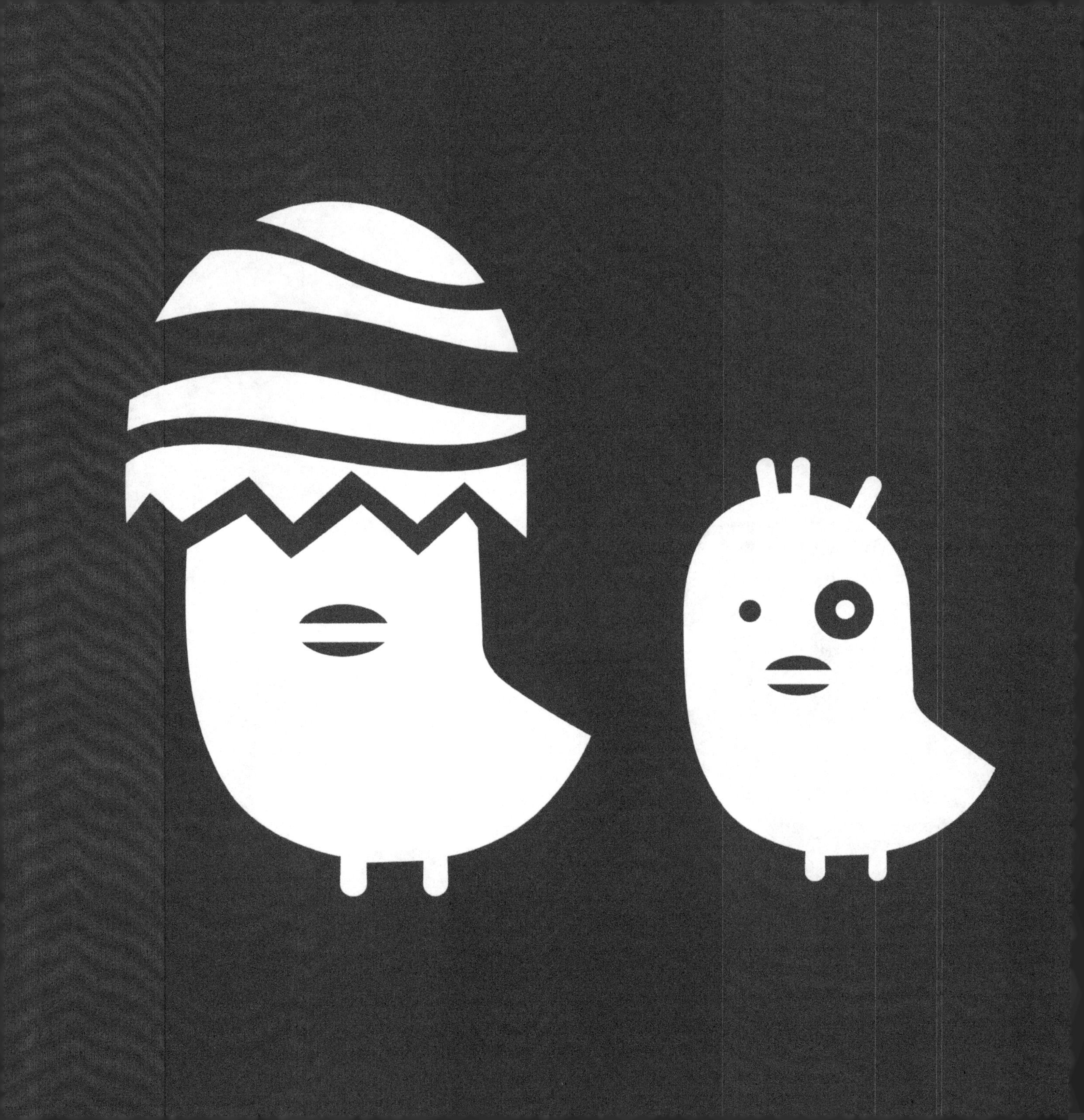

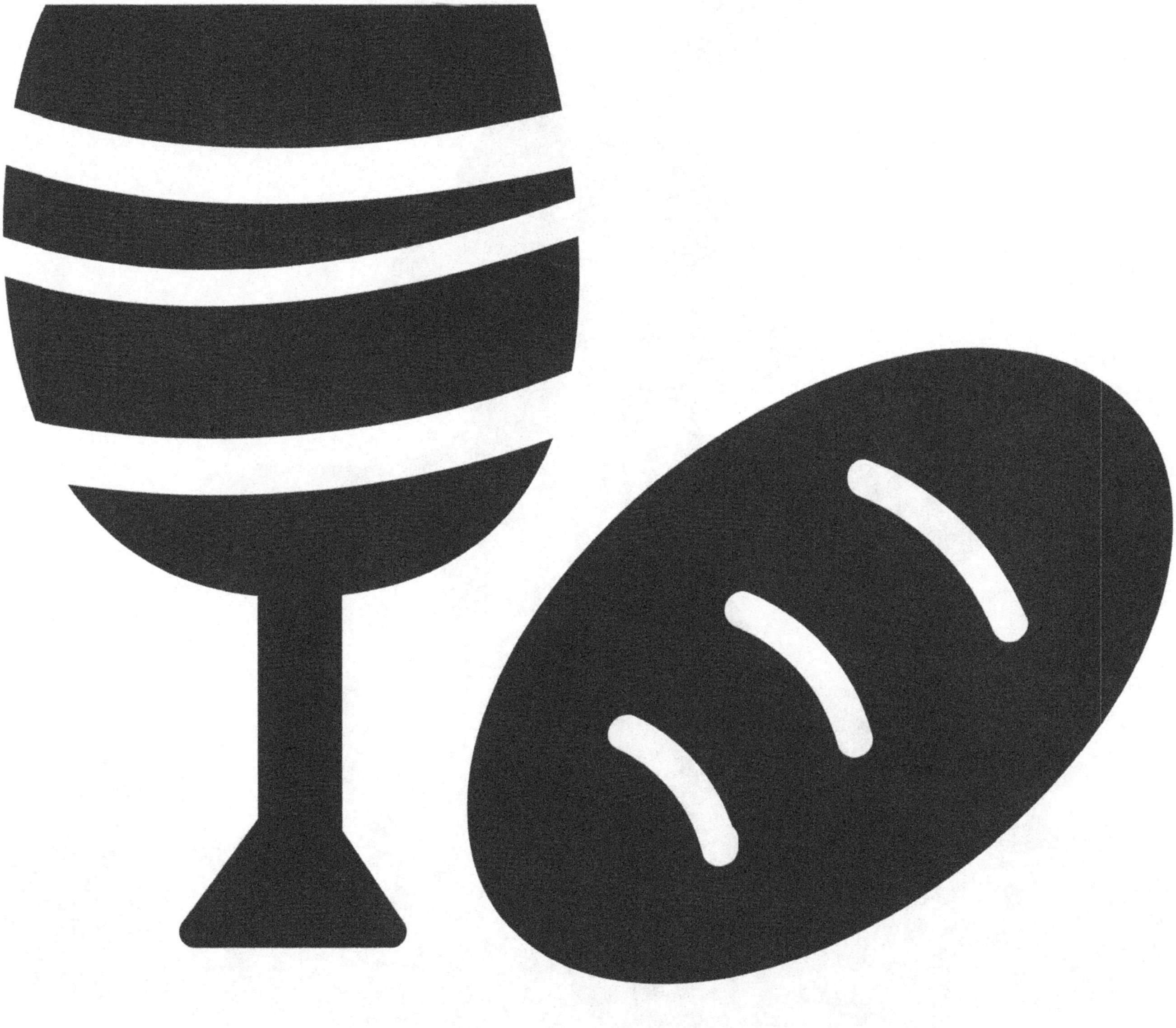

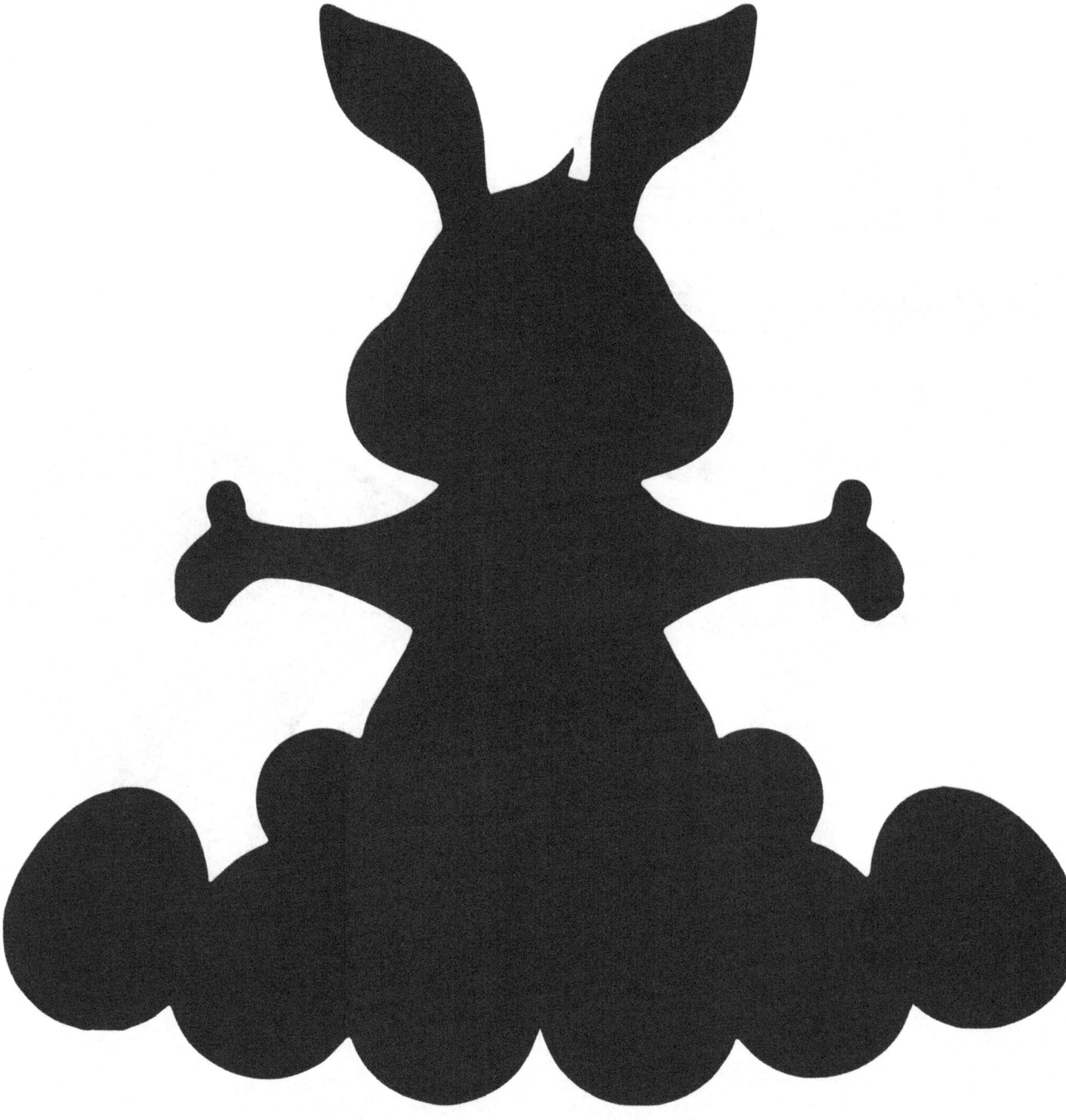

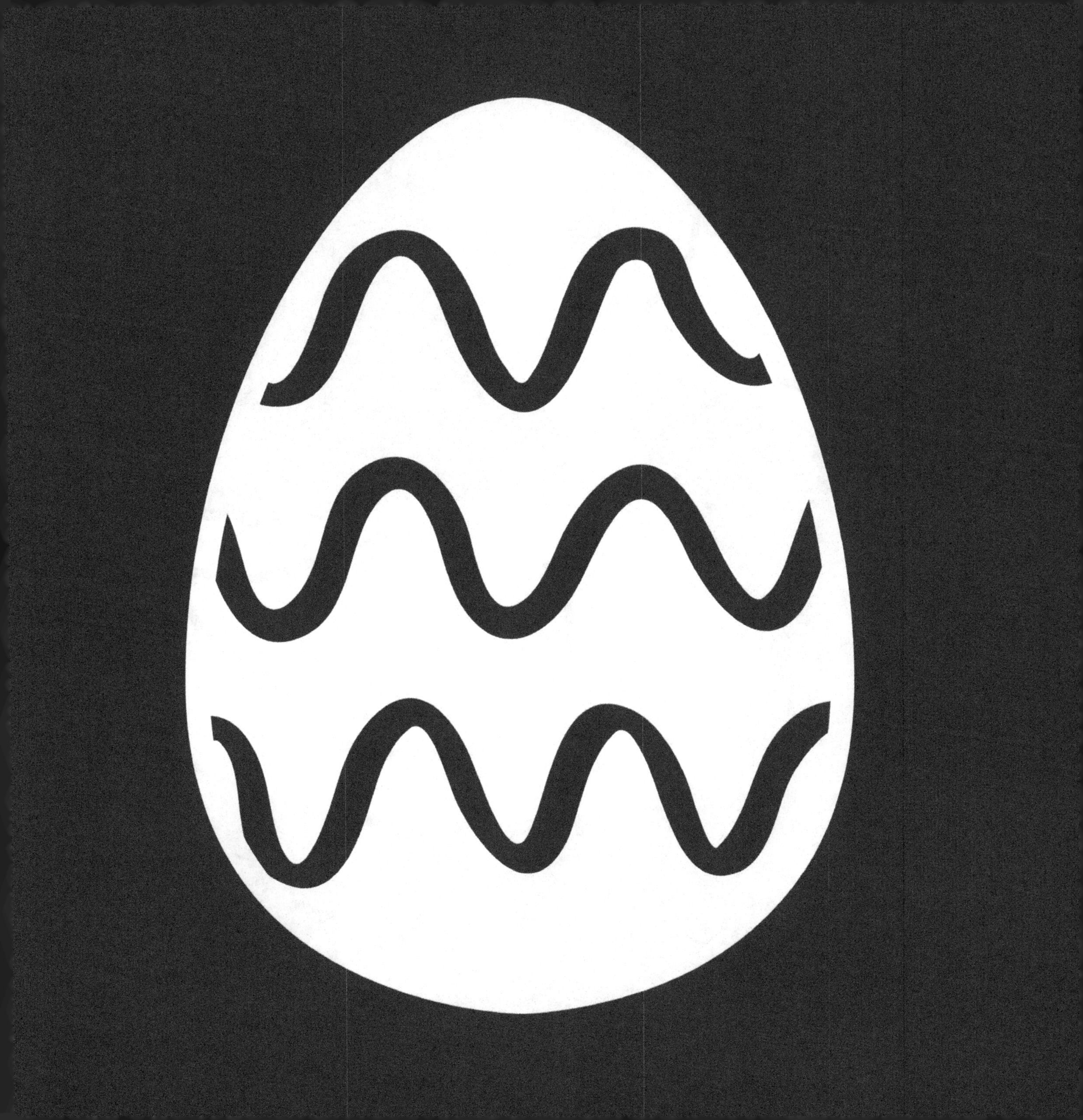

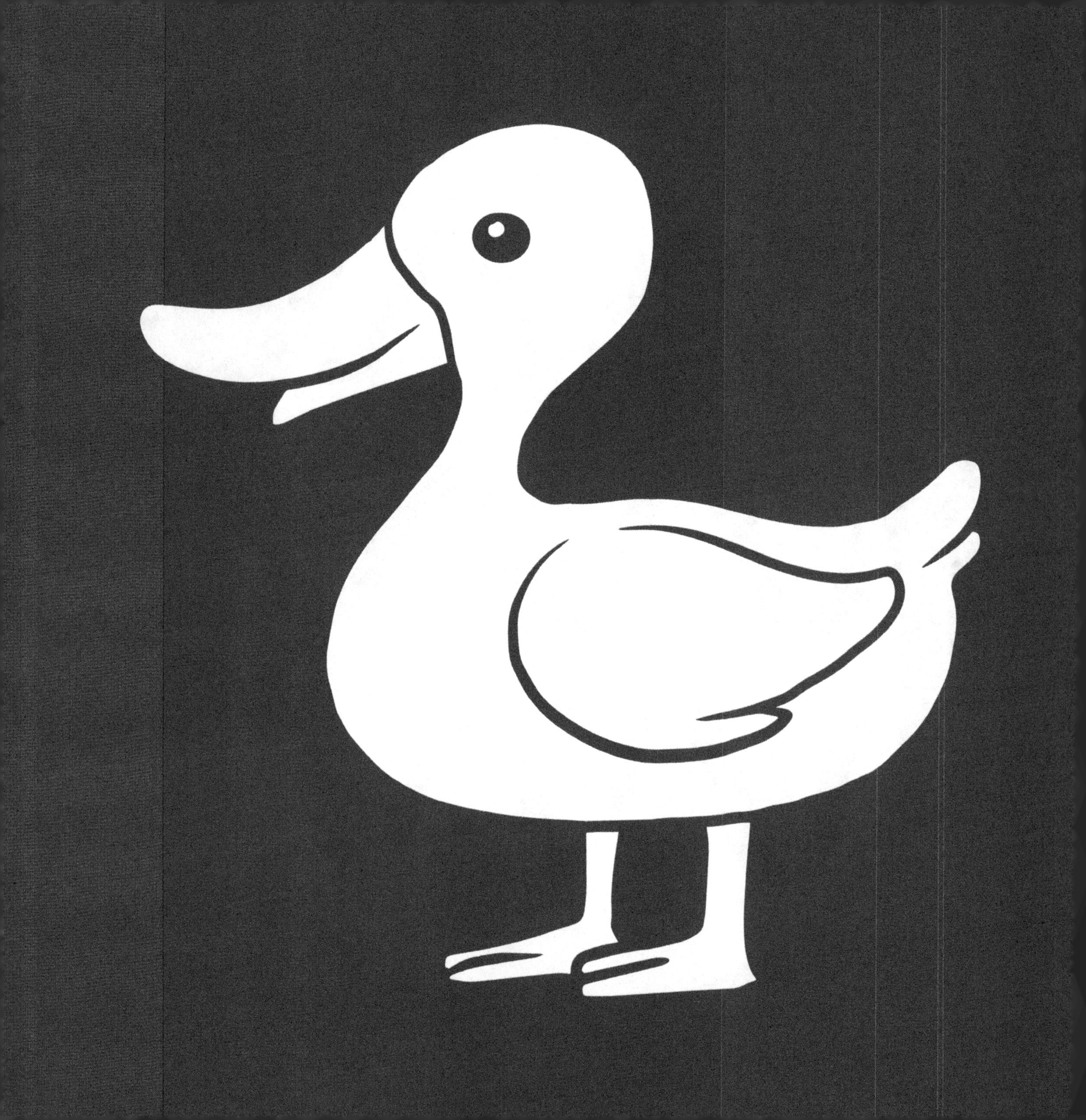

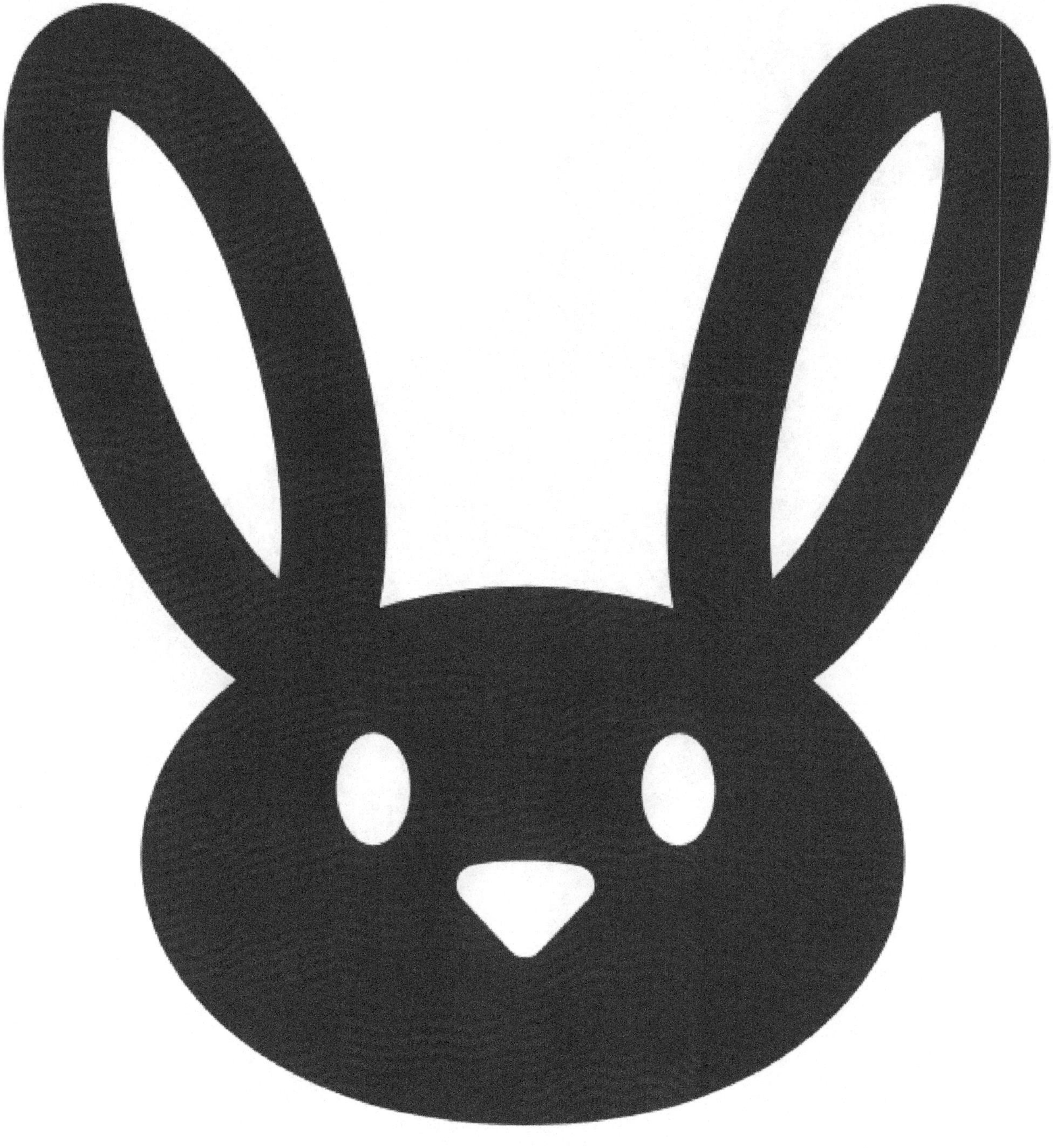

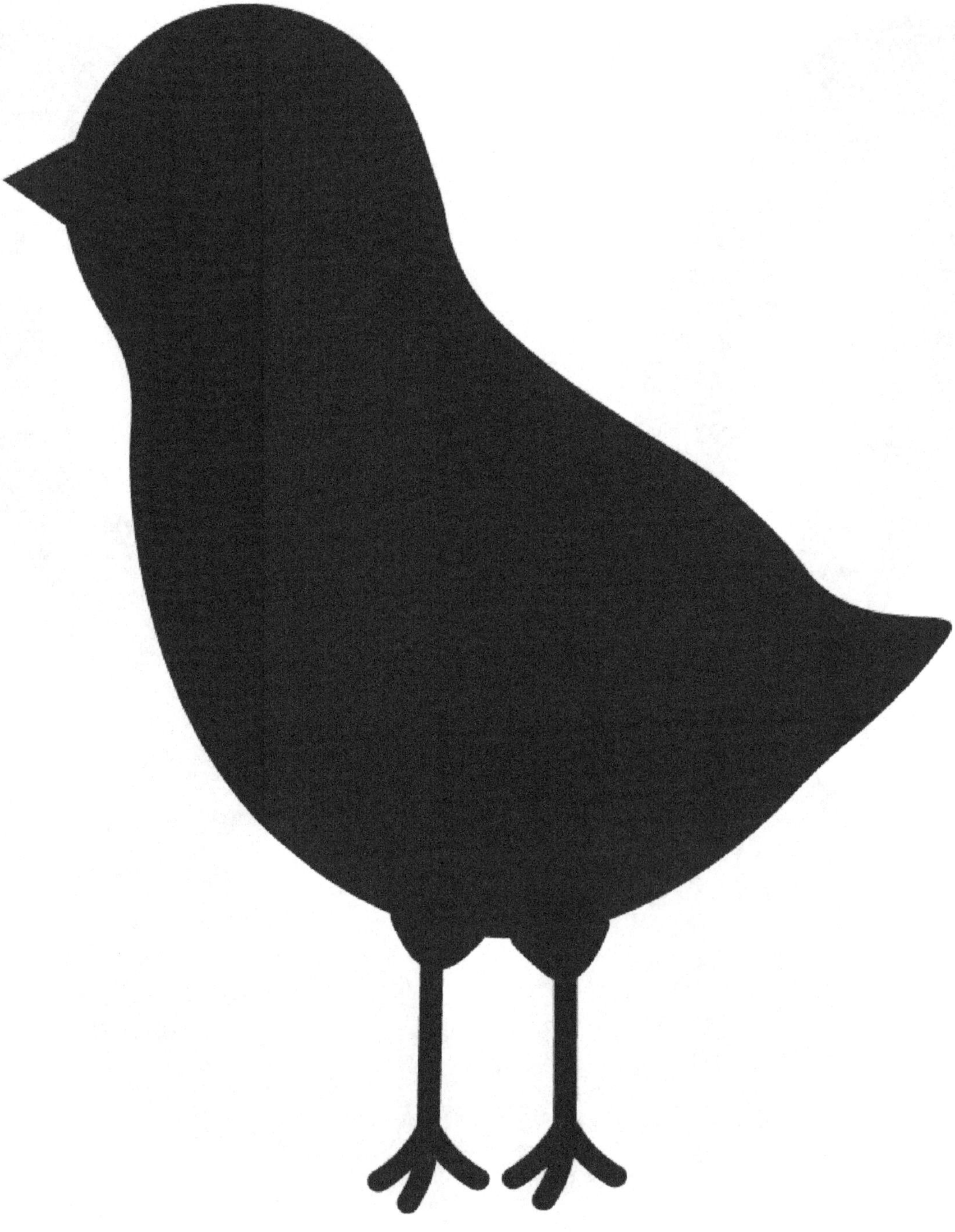

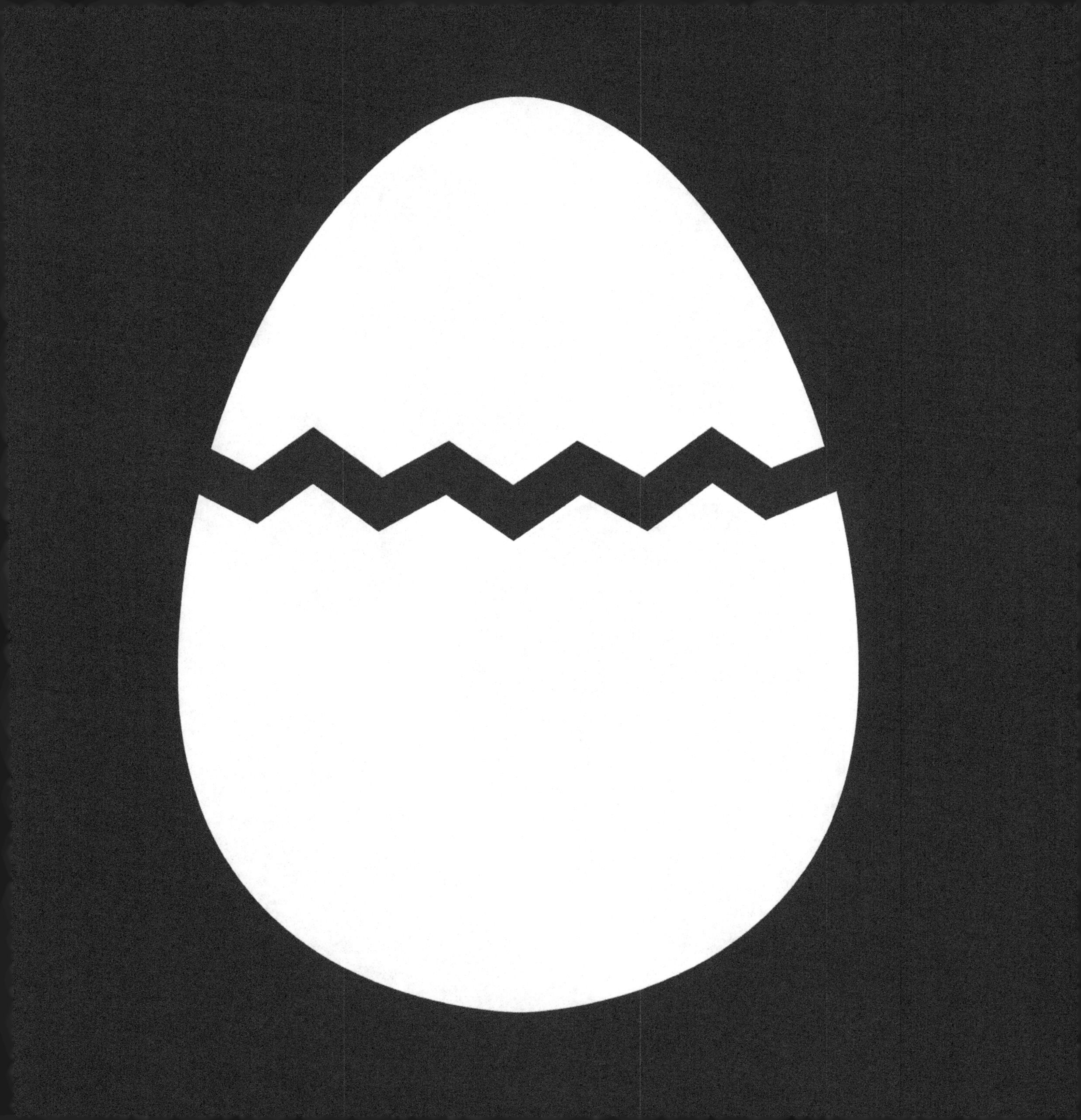

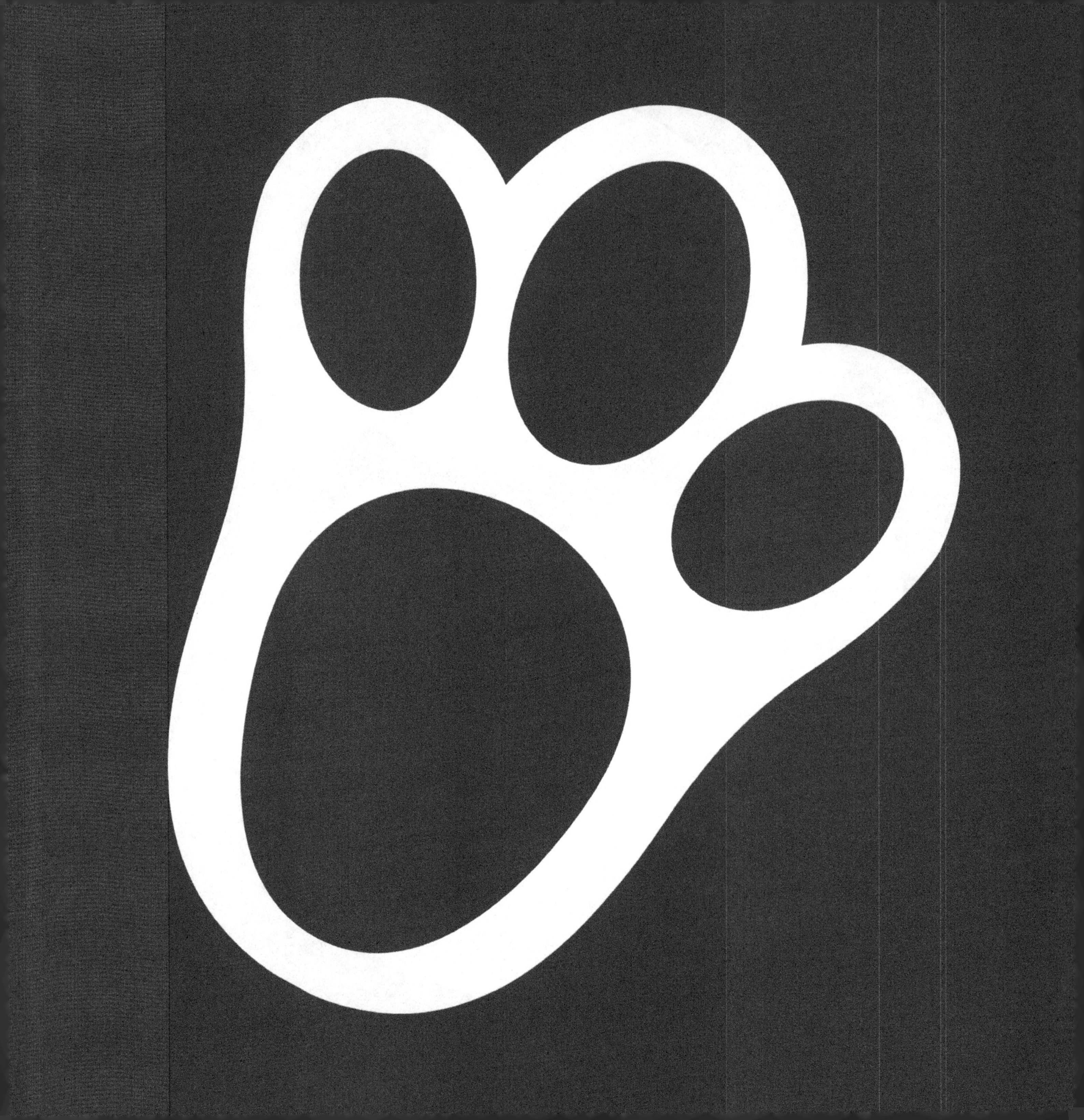

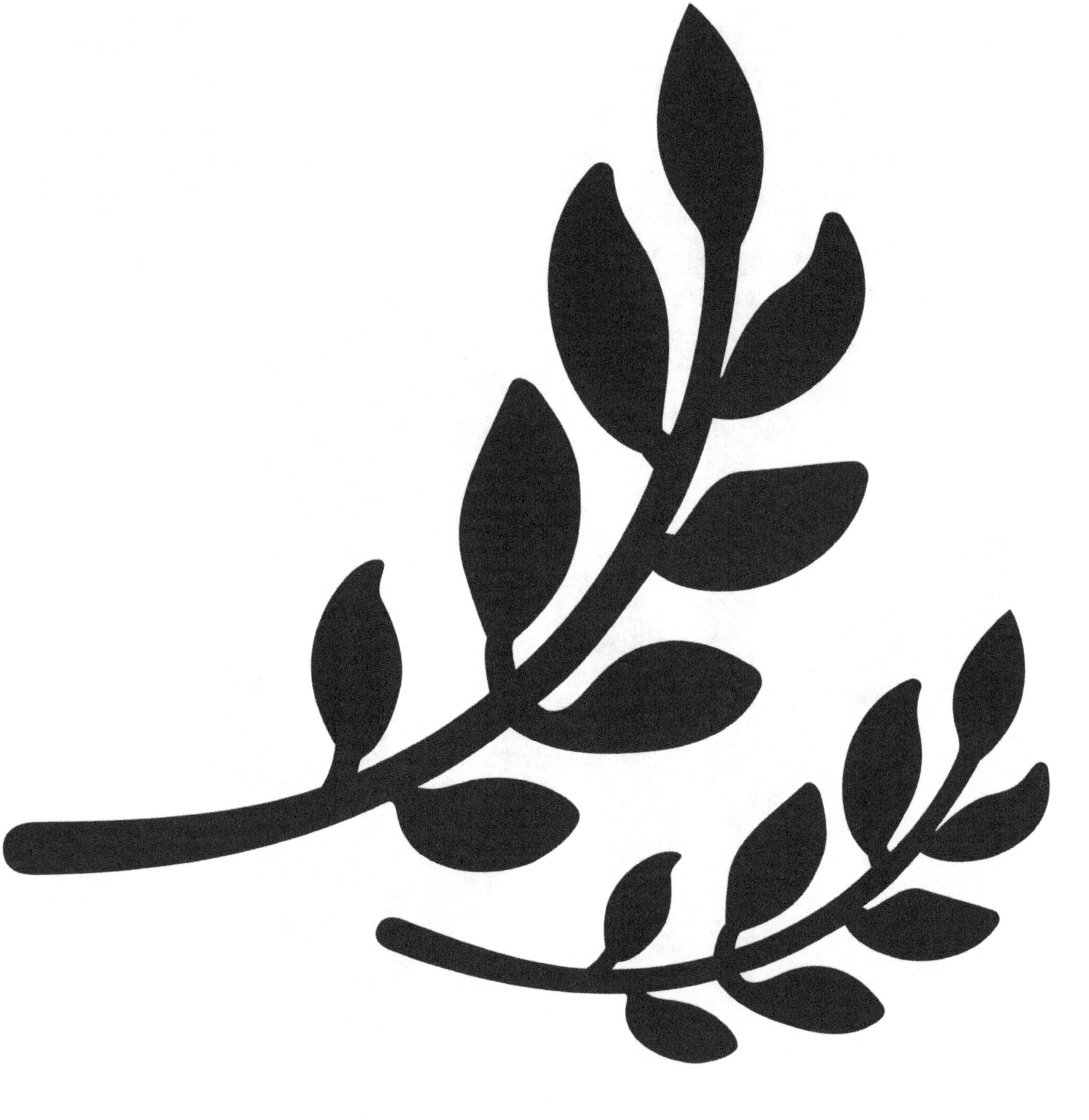

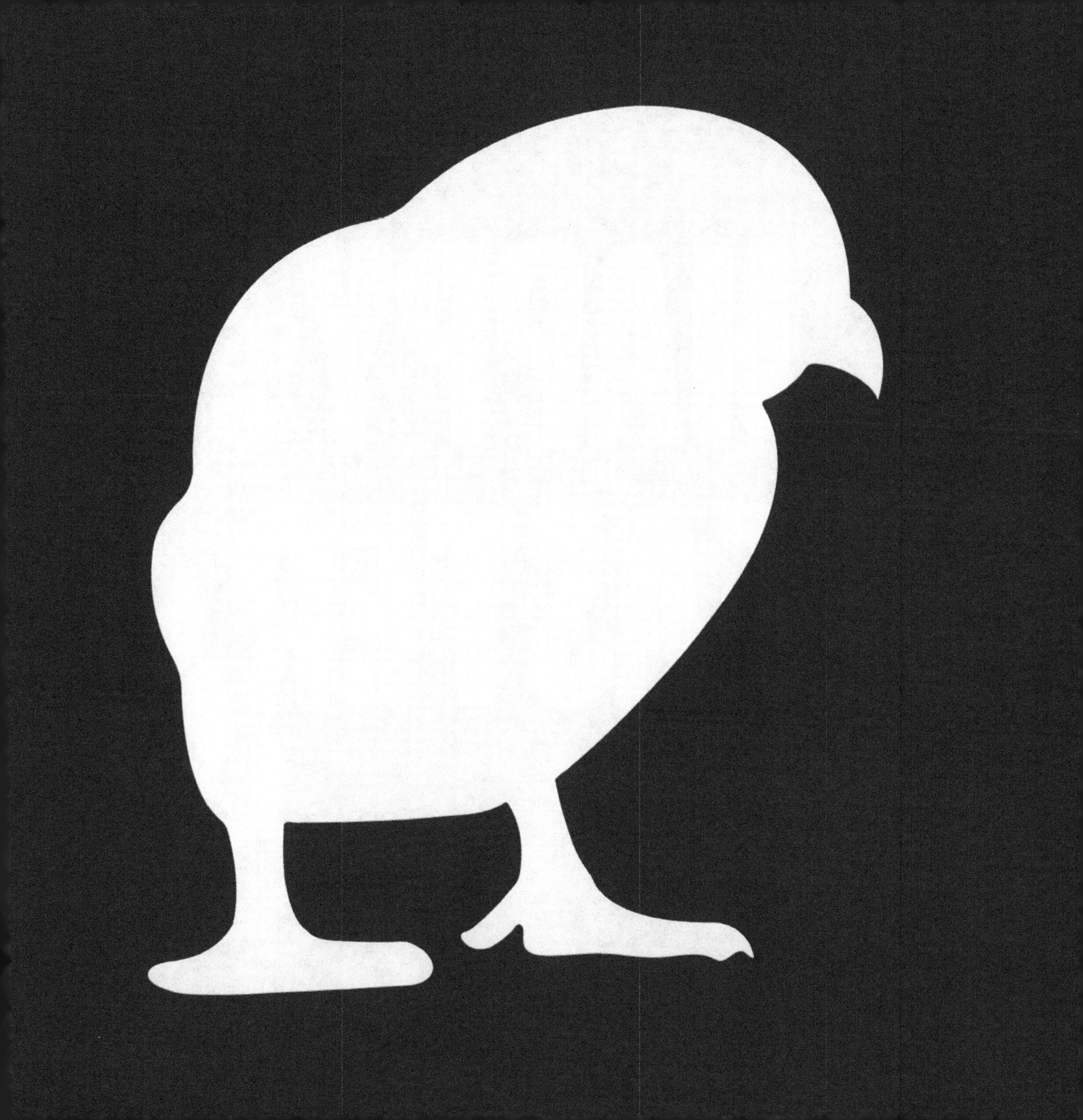

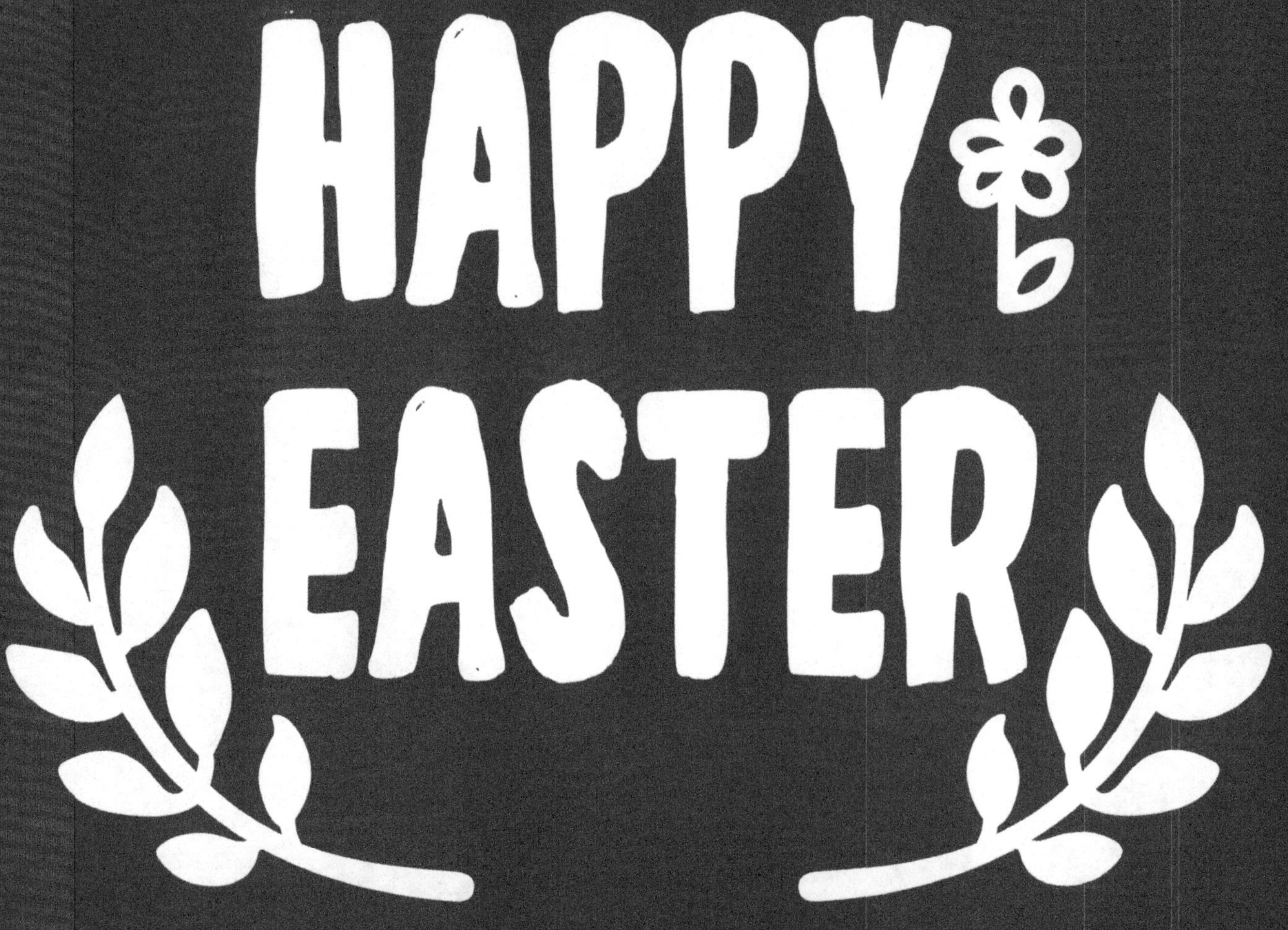
HAPPY
EASTER

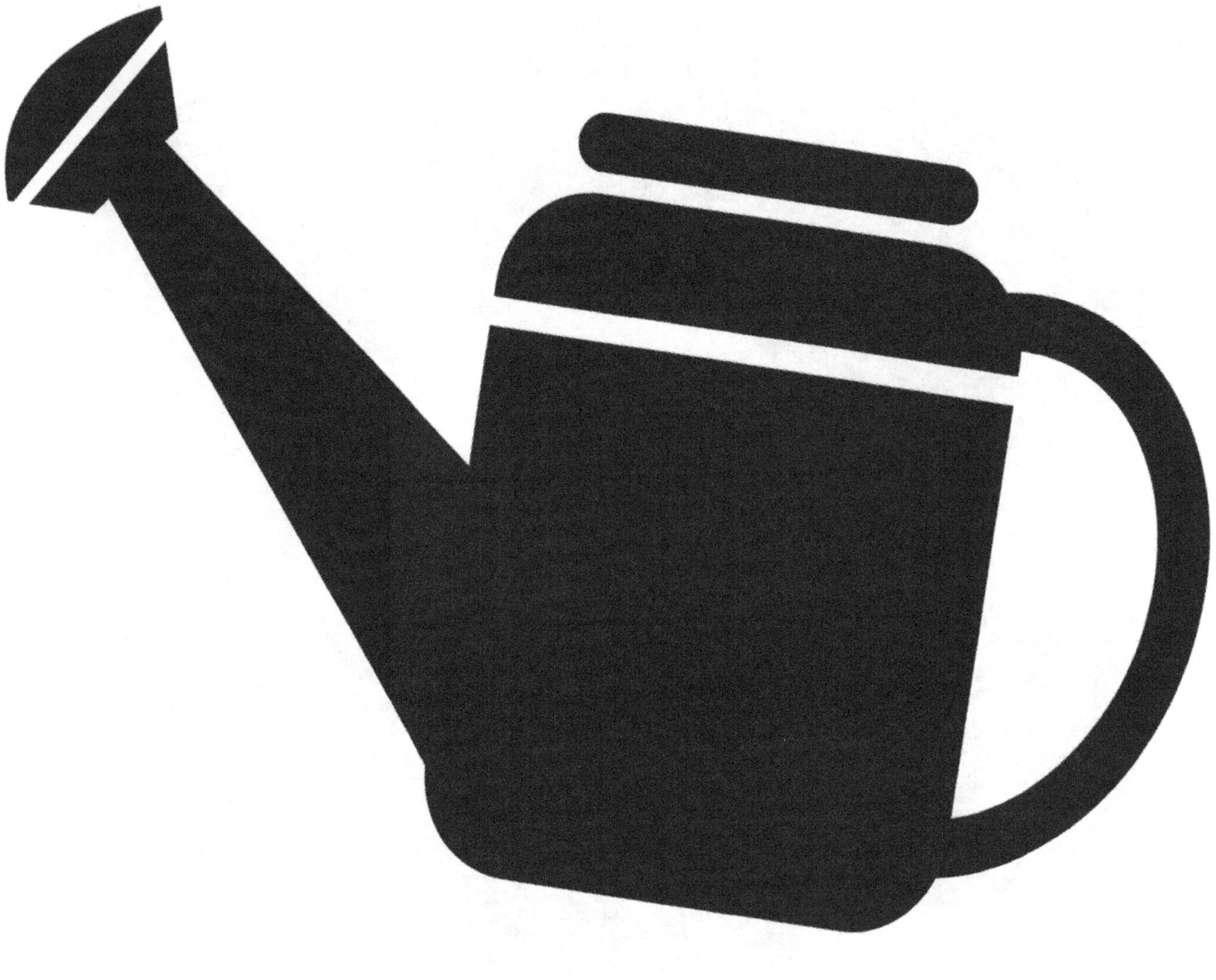

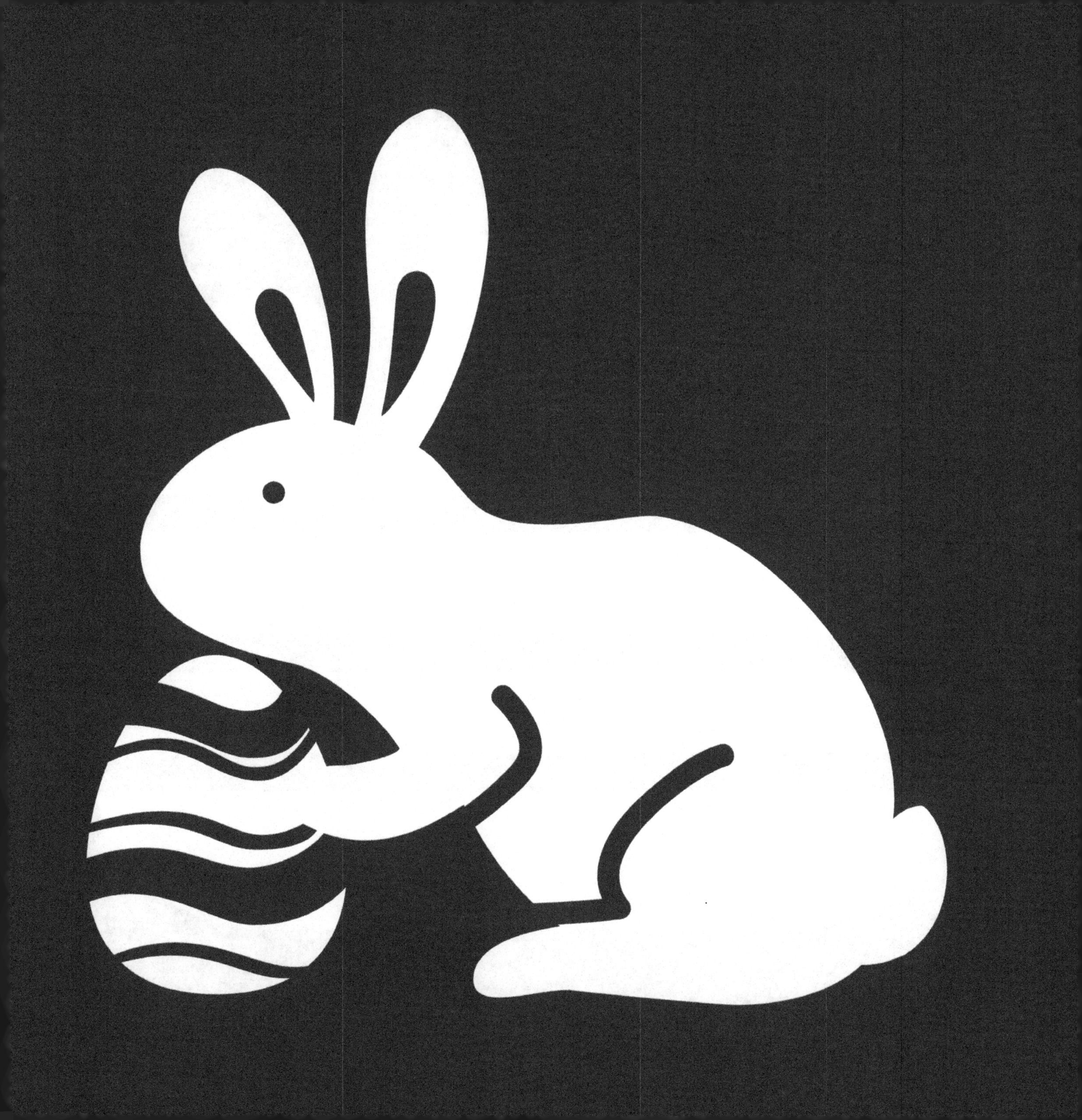

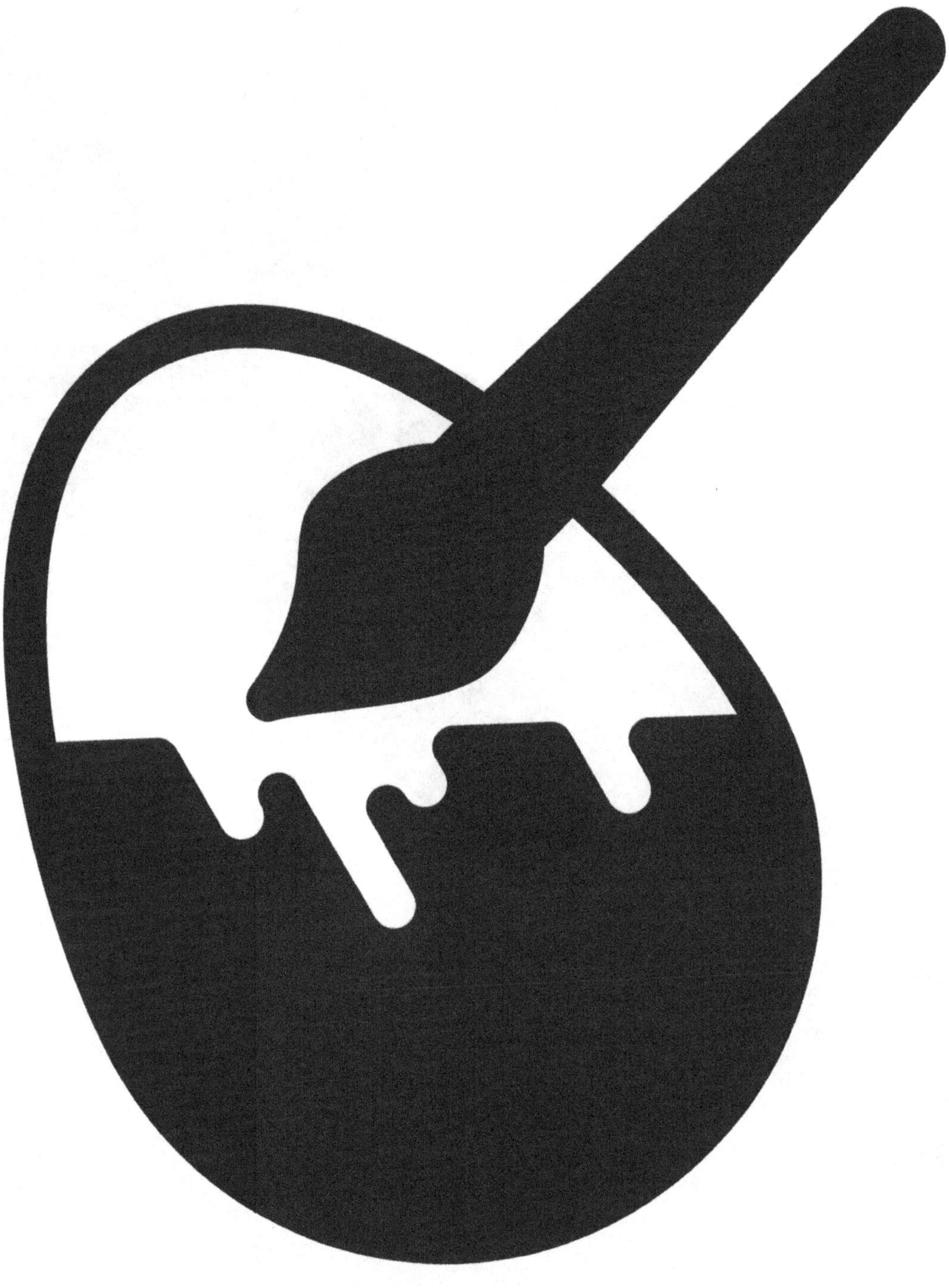

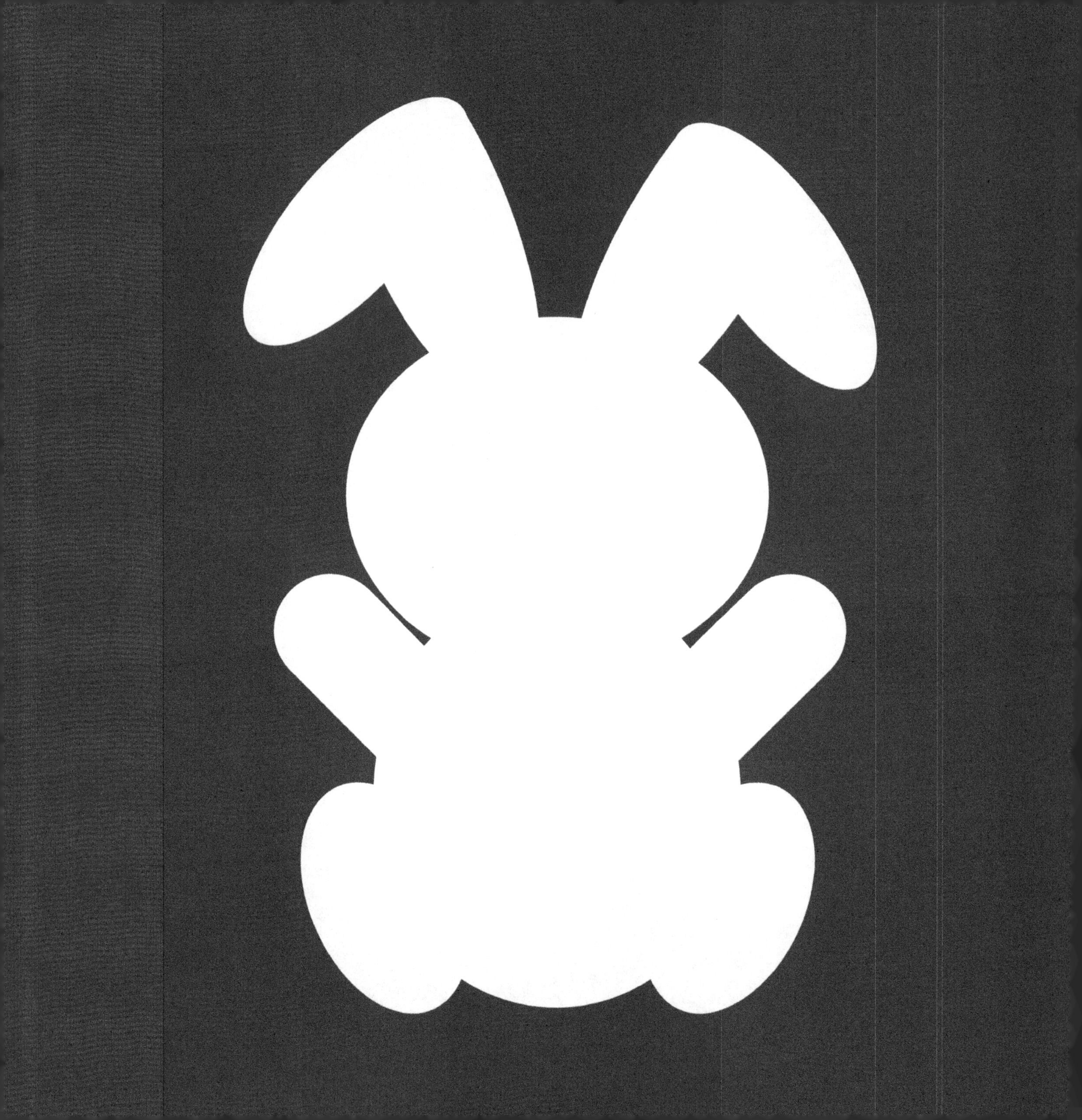

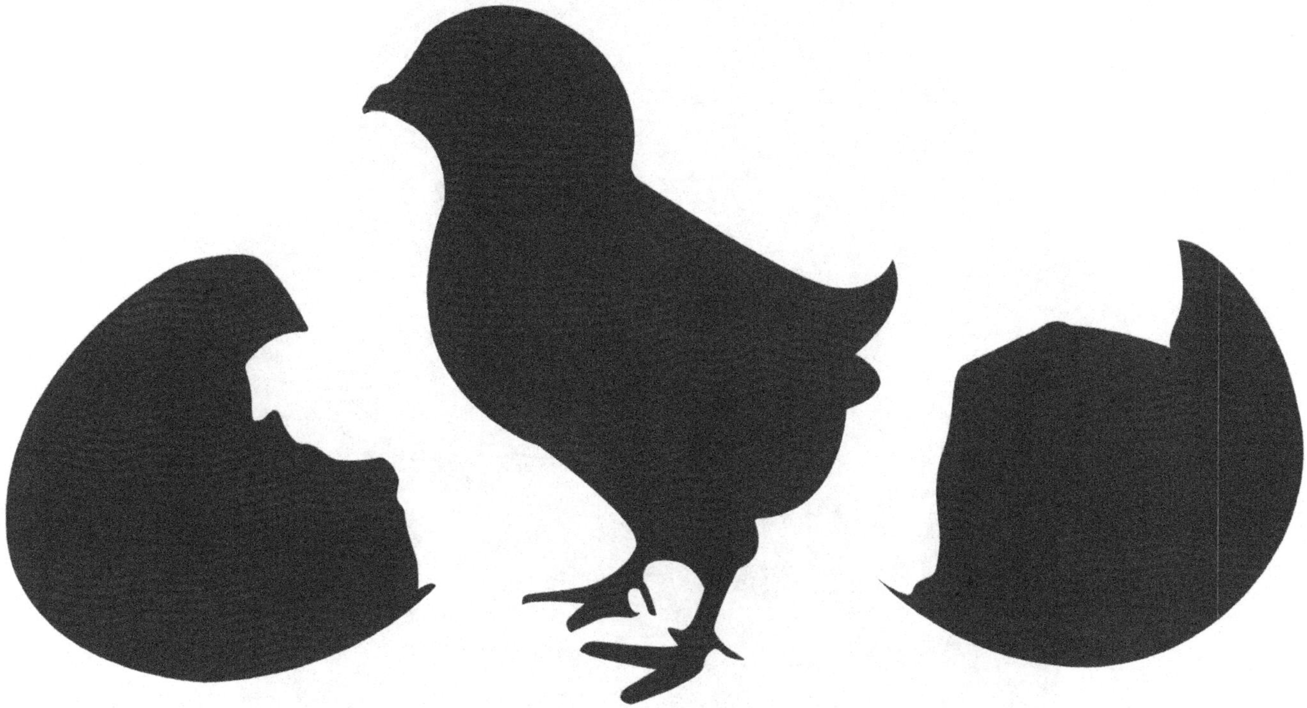

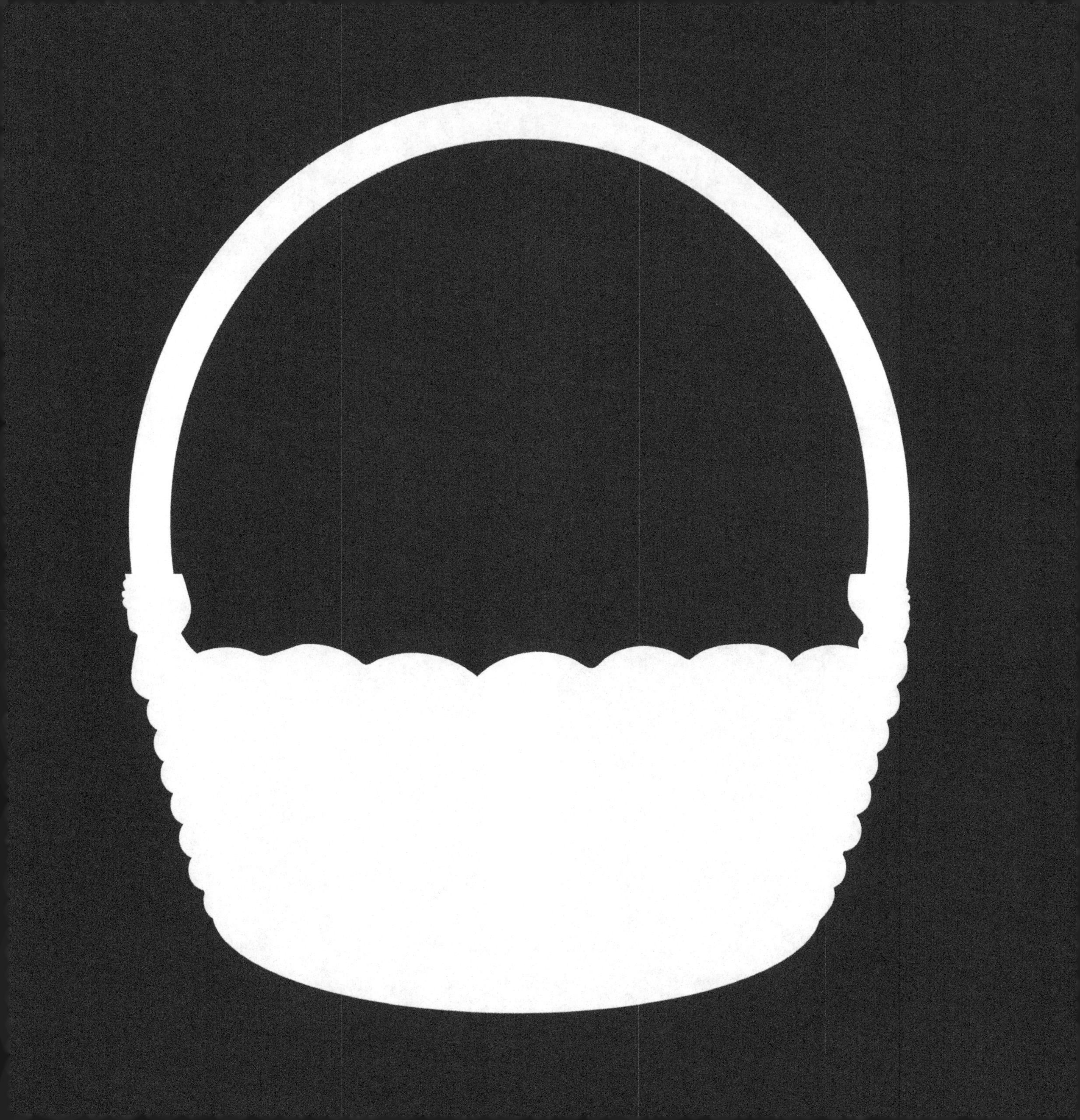

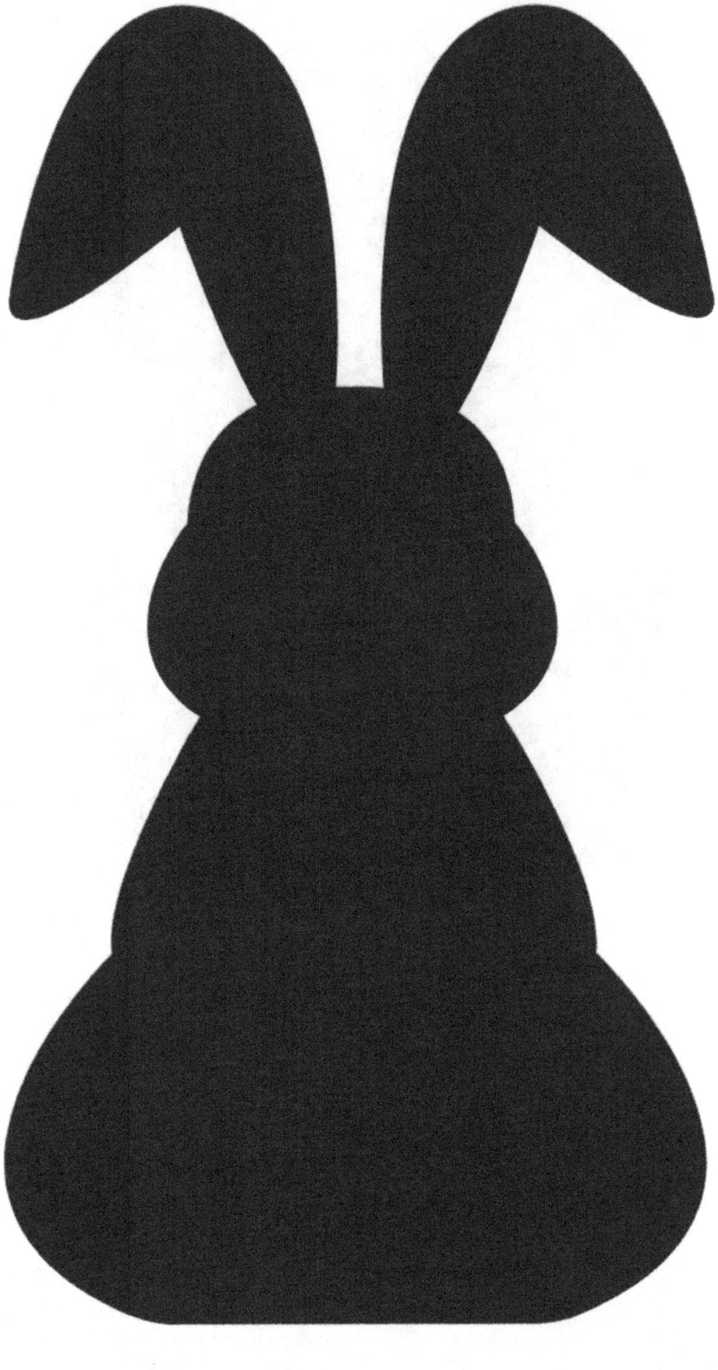

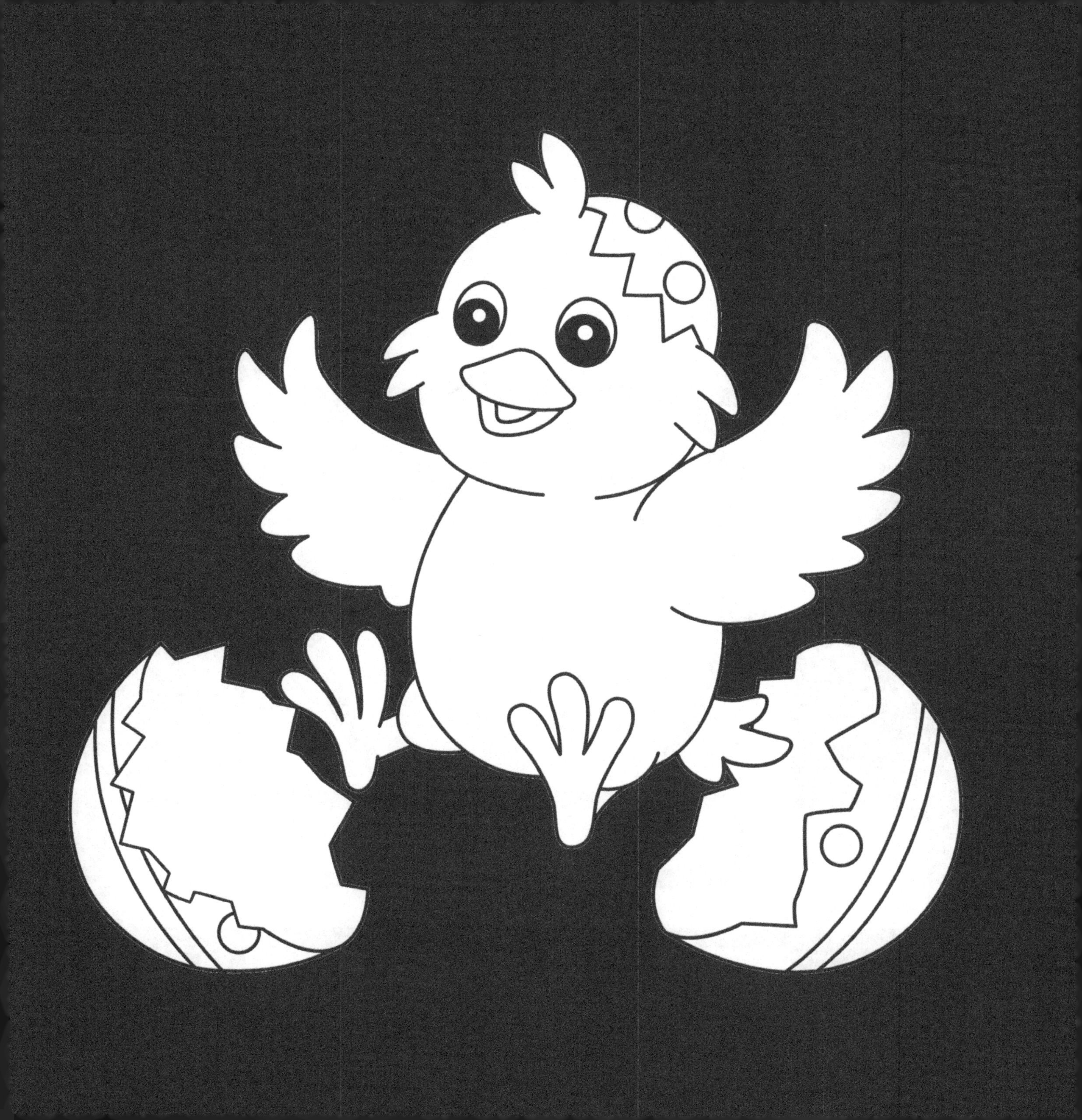

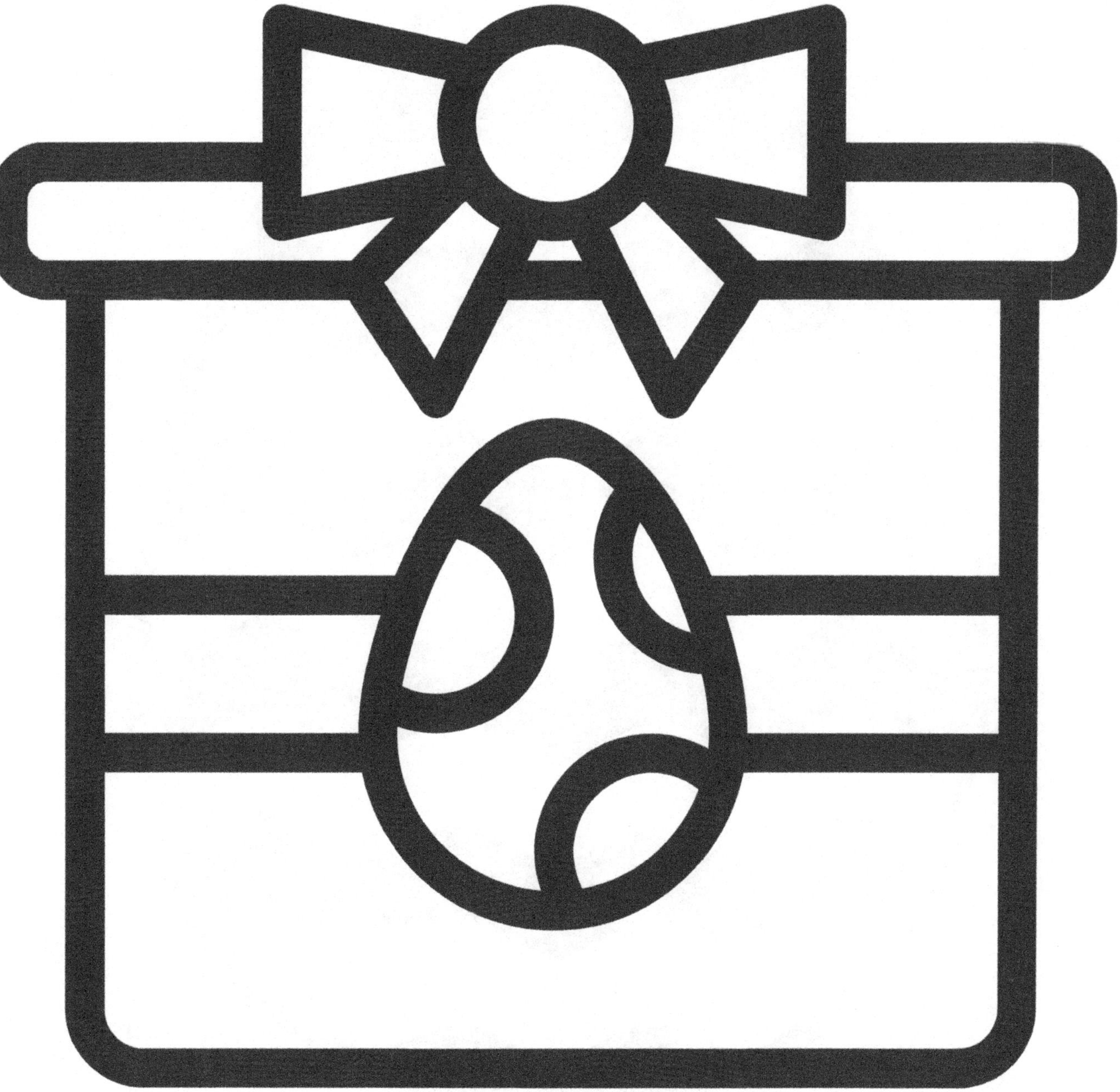

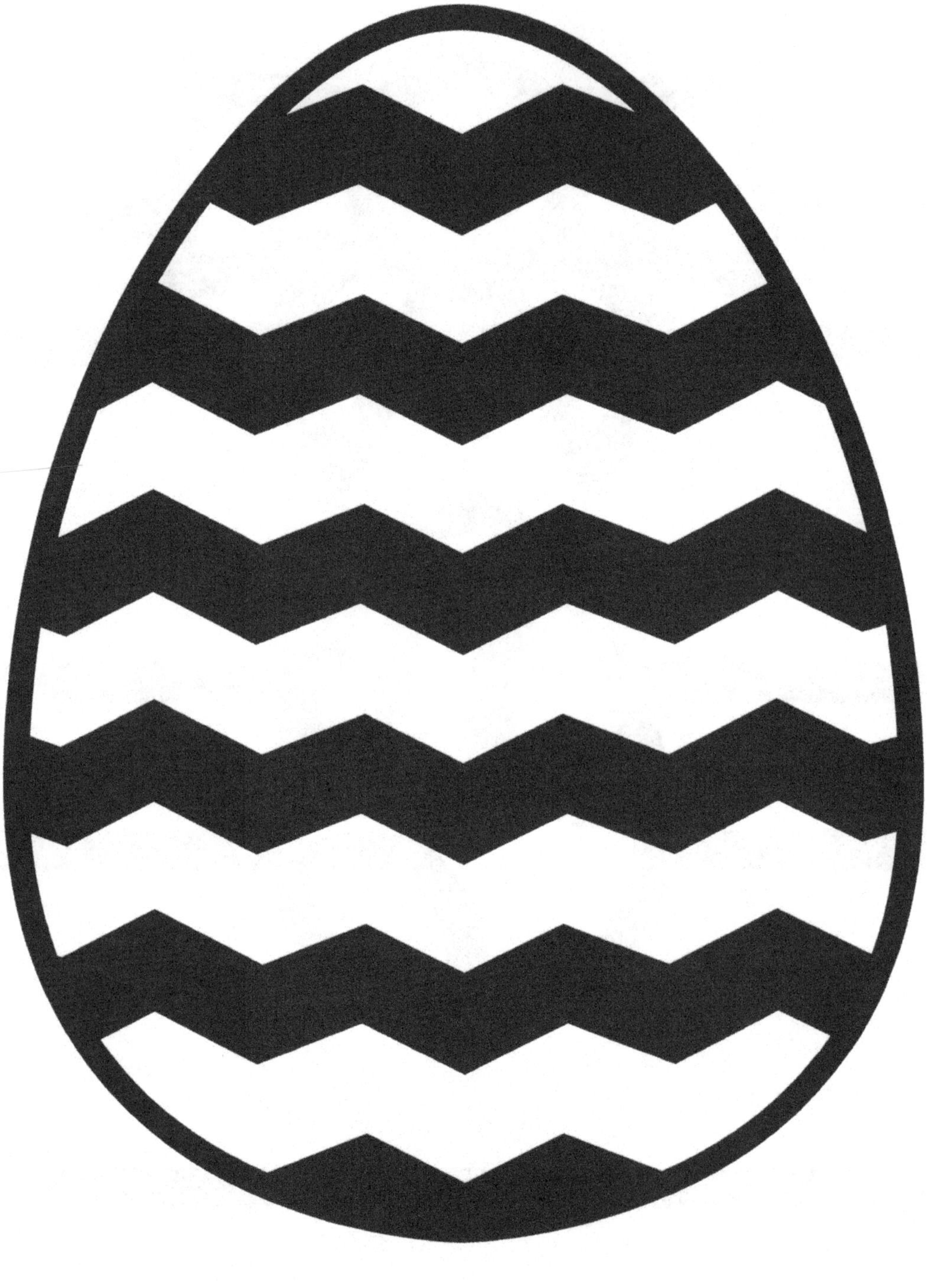

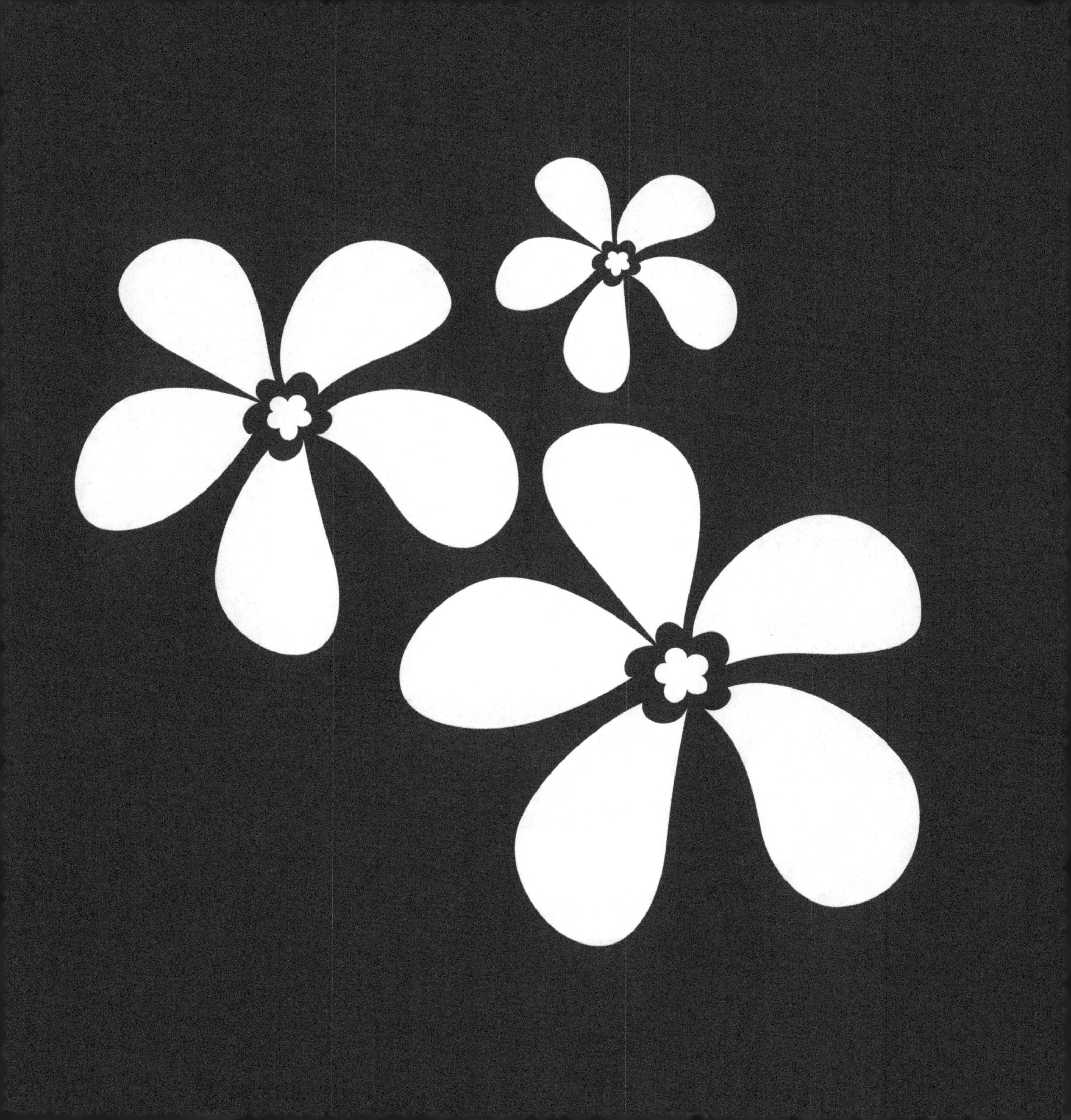

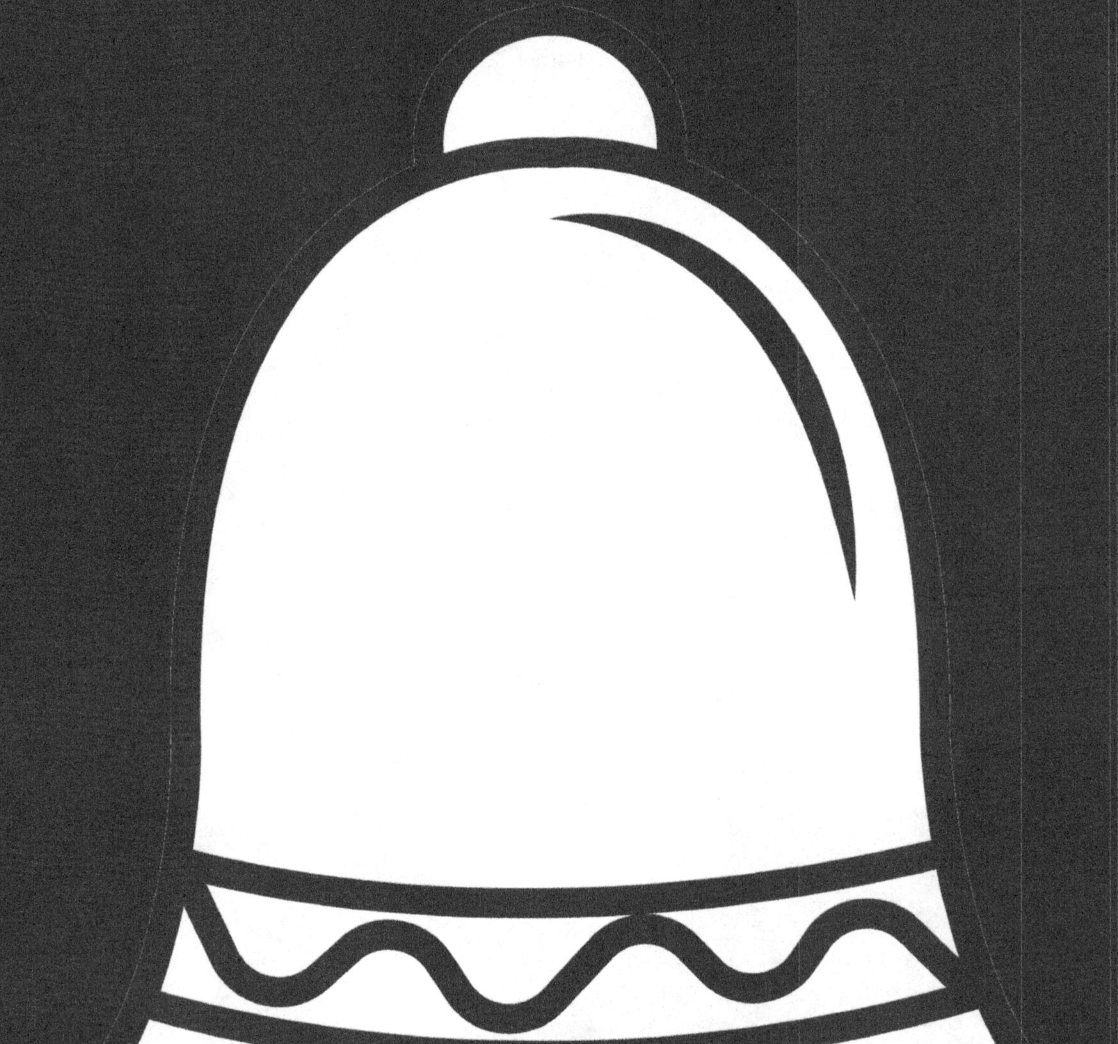

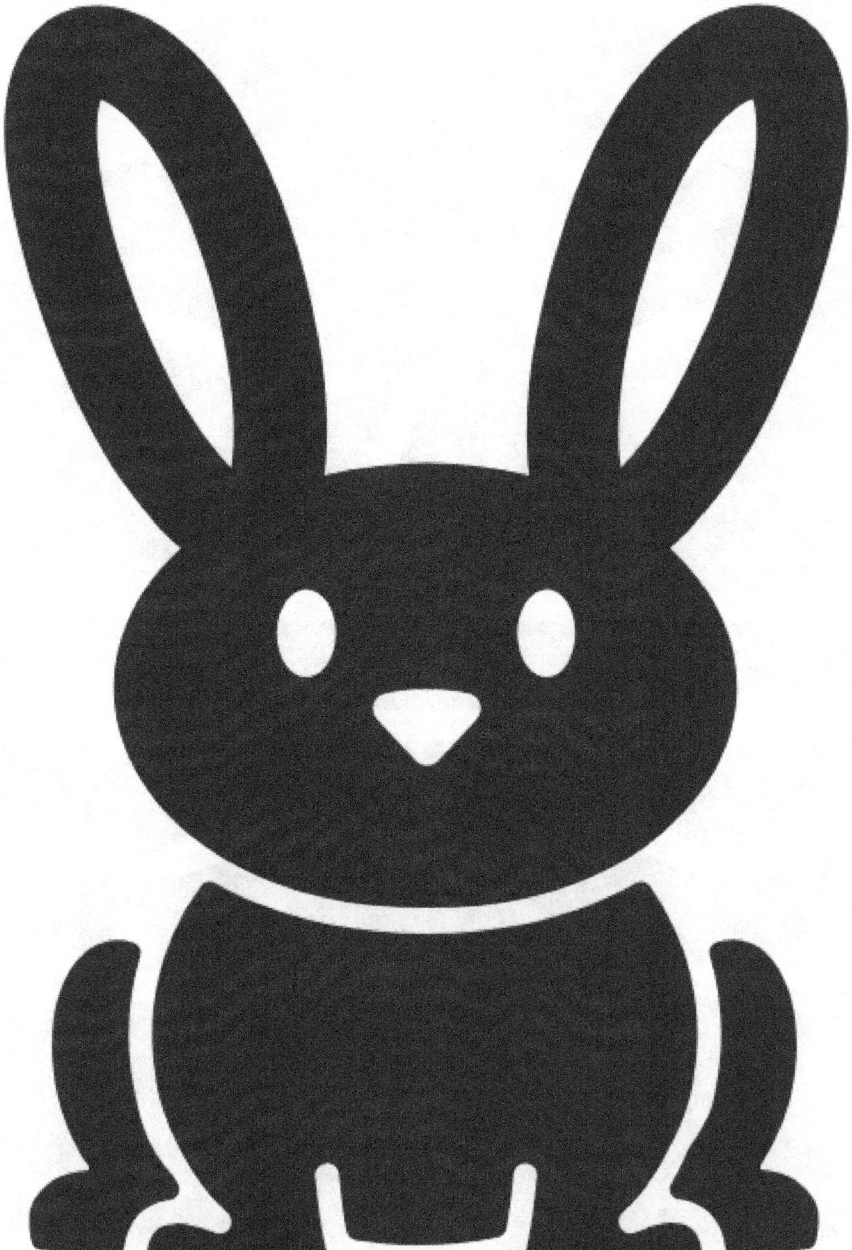

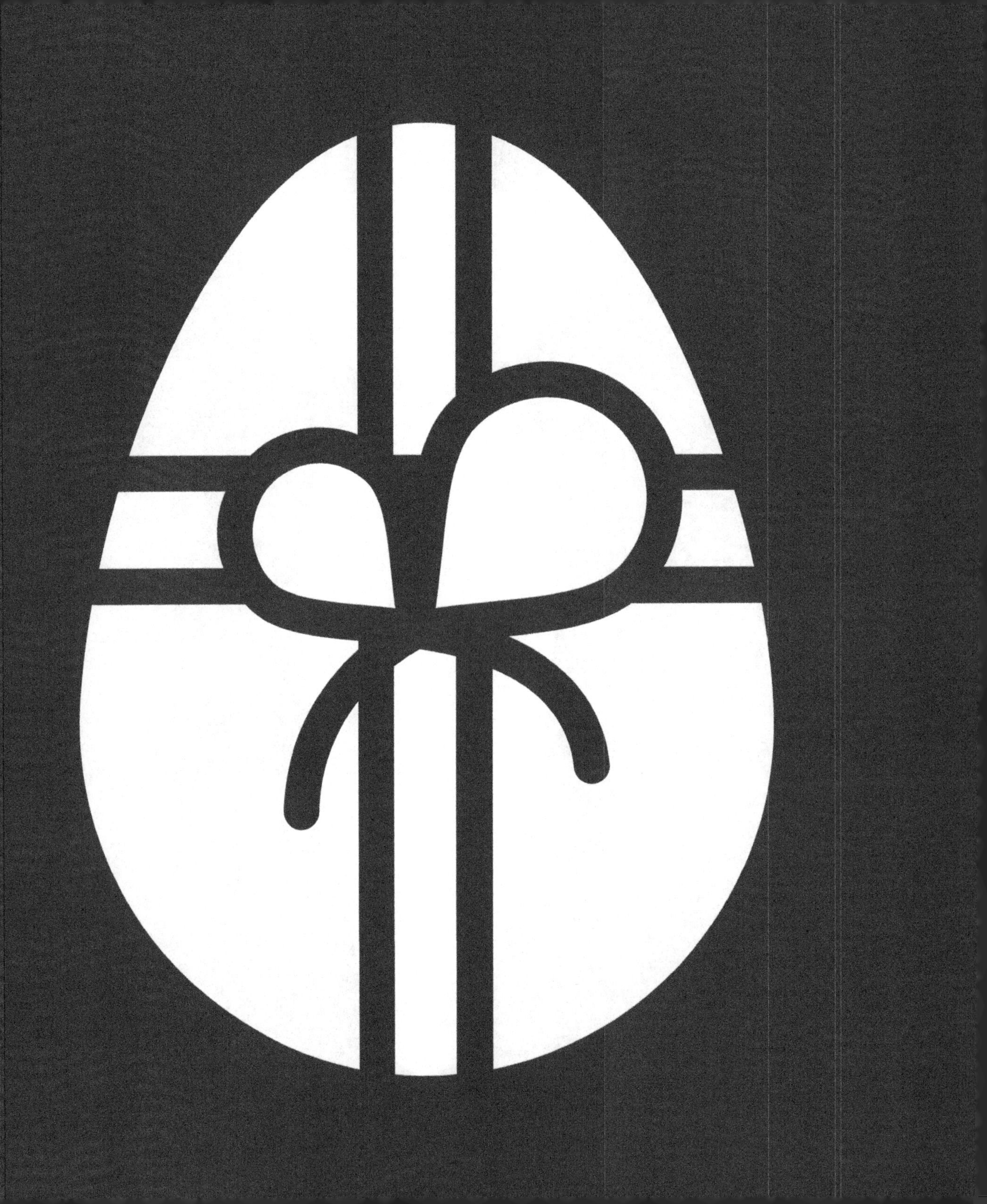

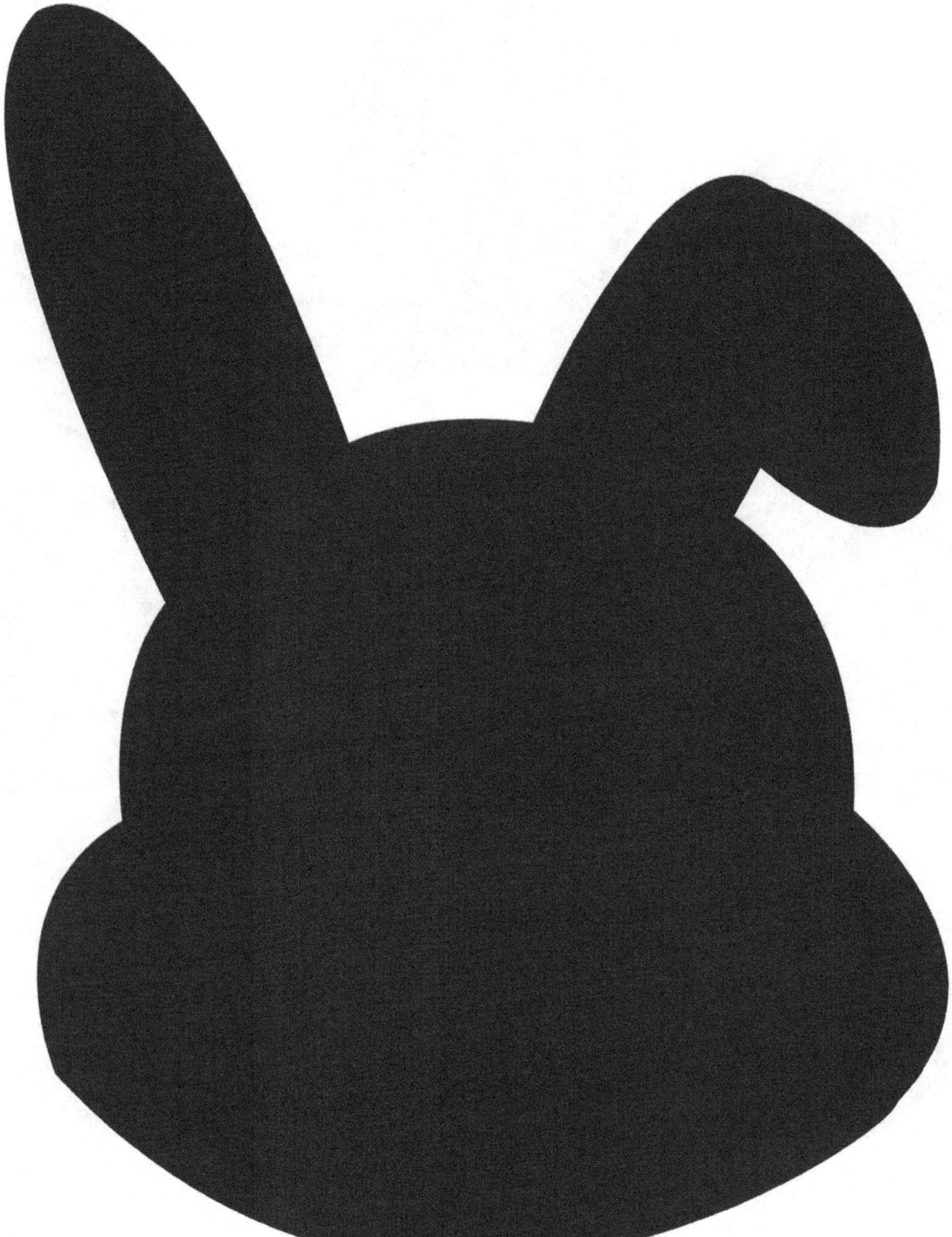

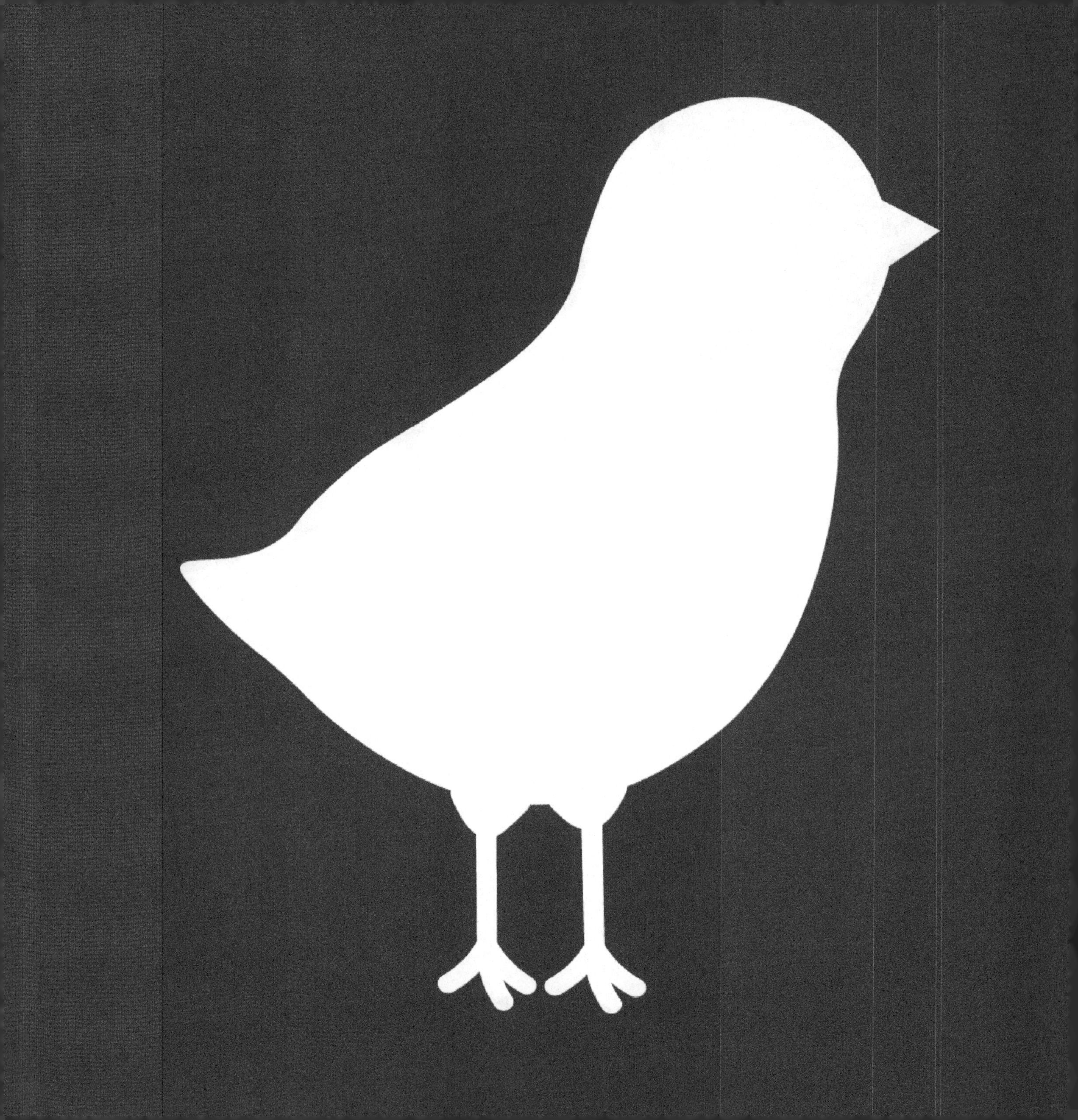

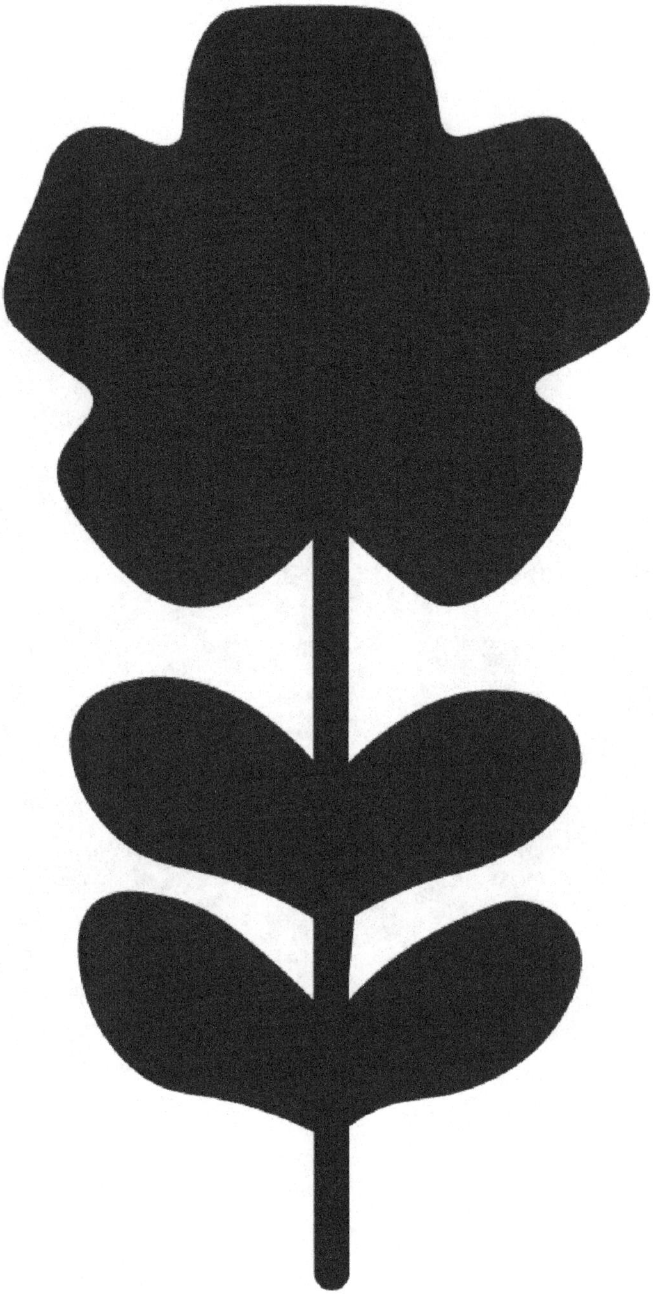

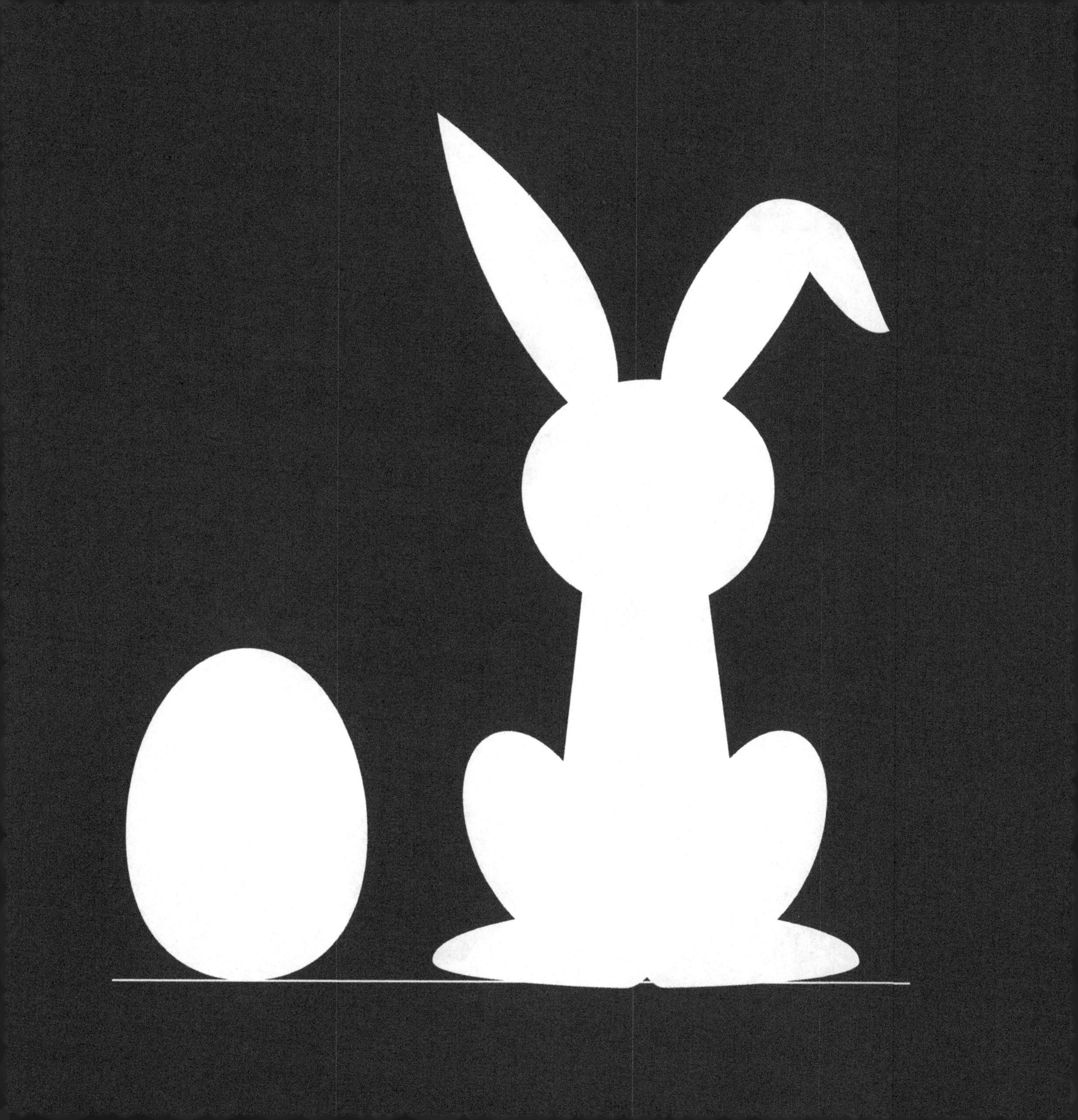

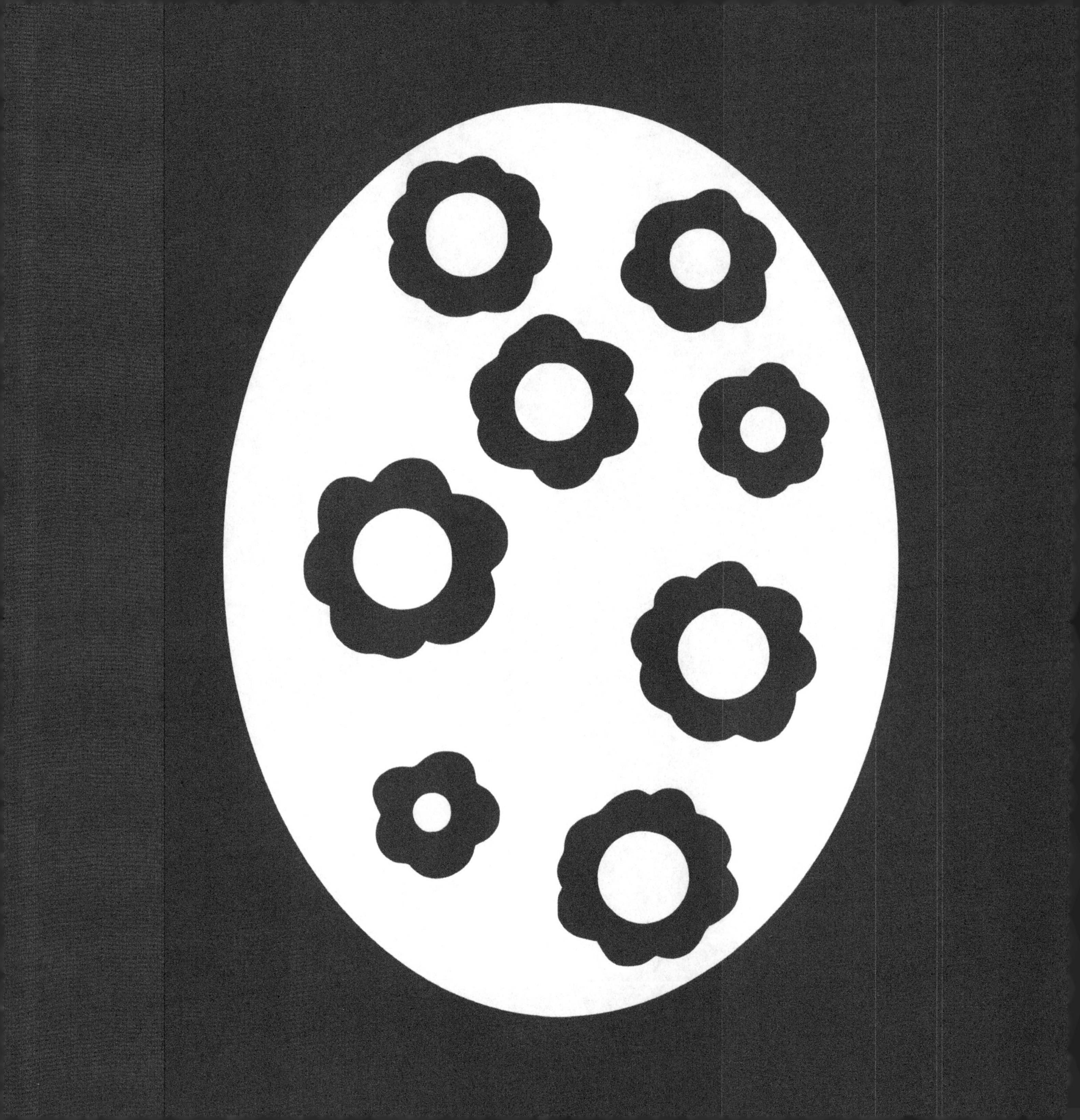

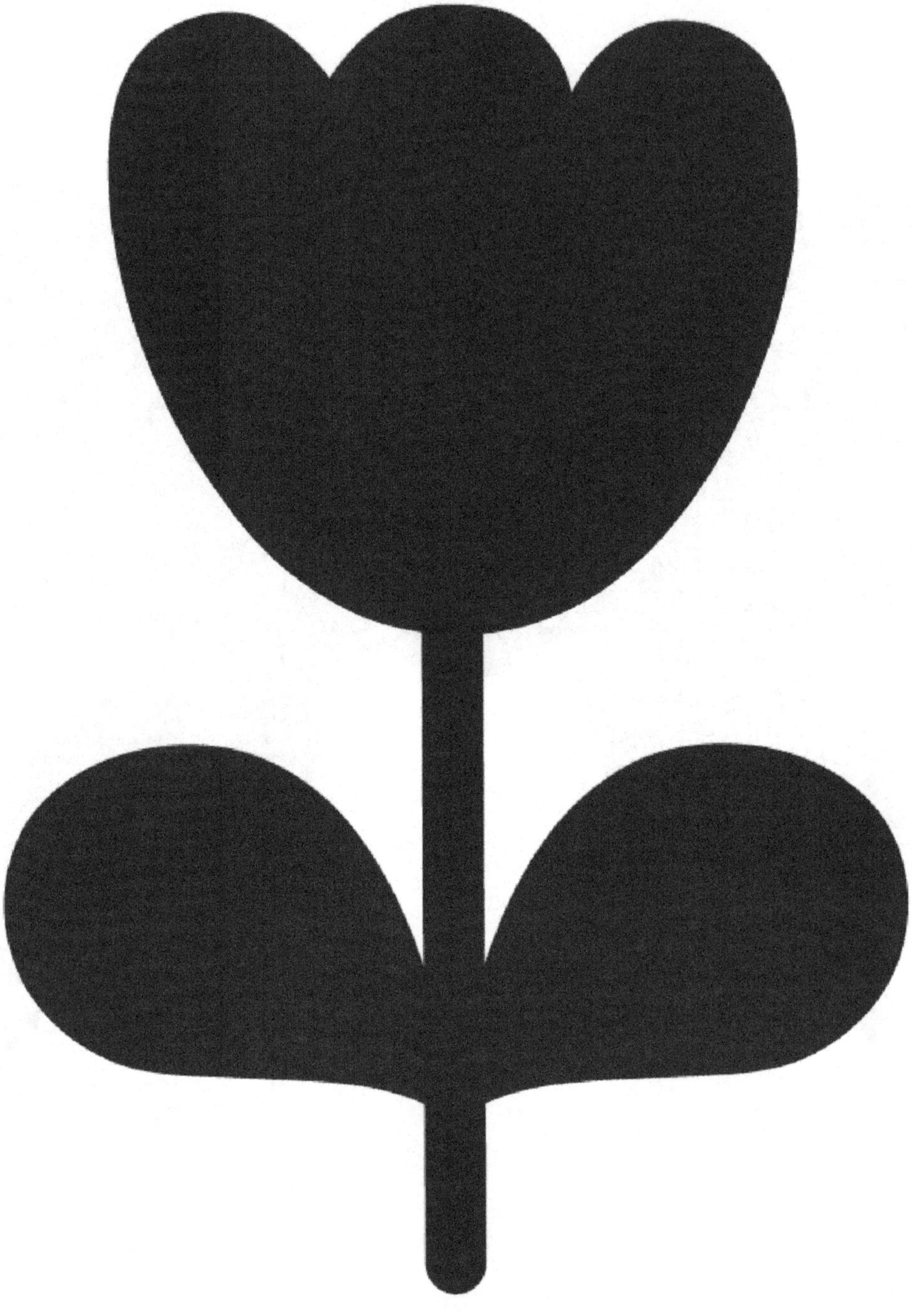

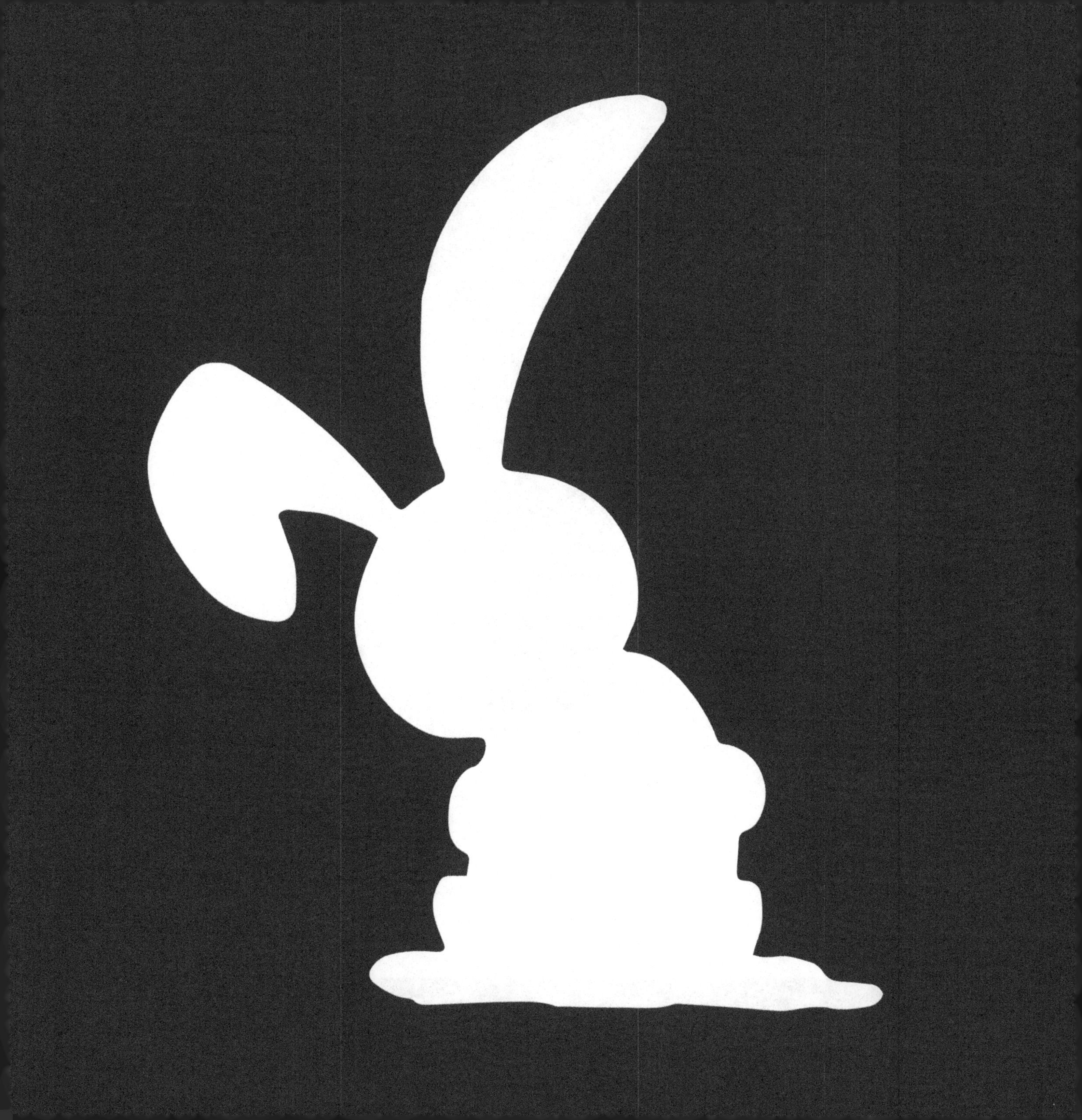

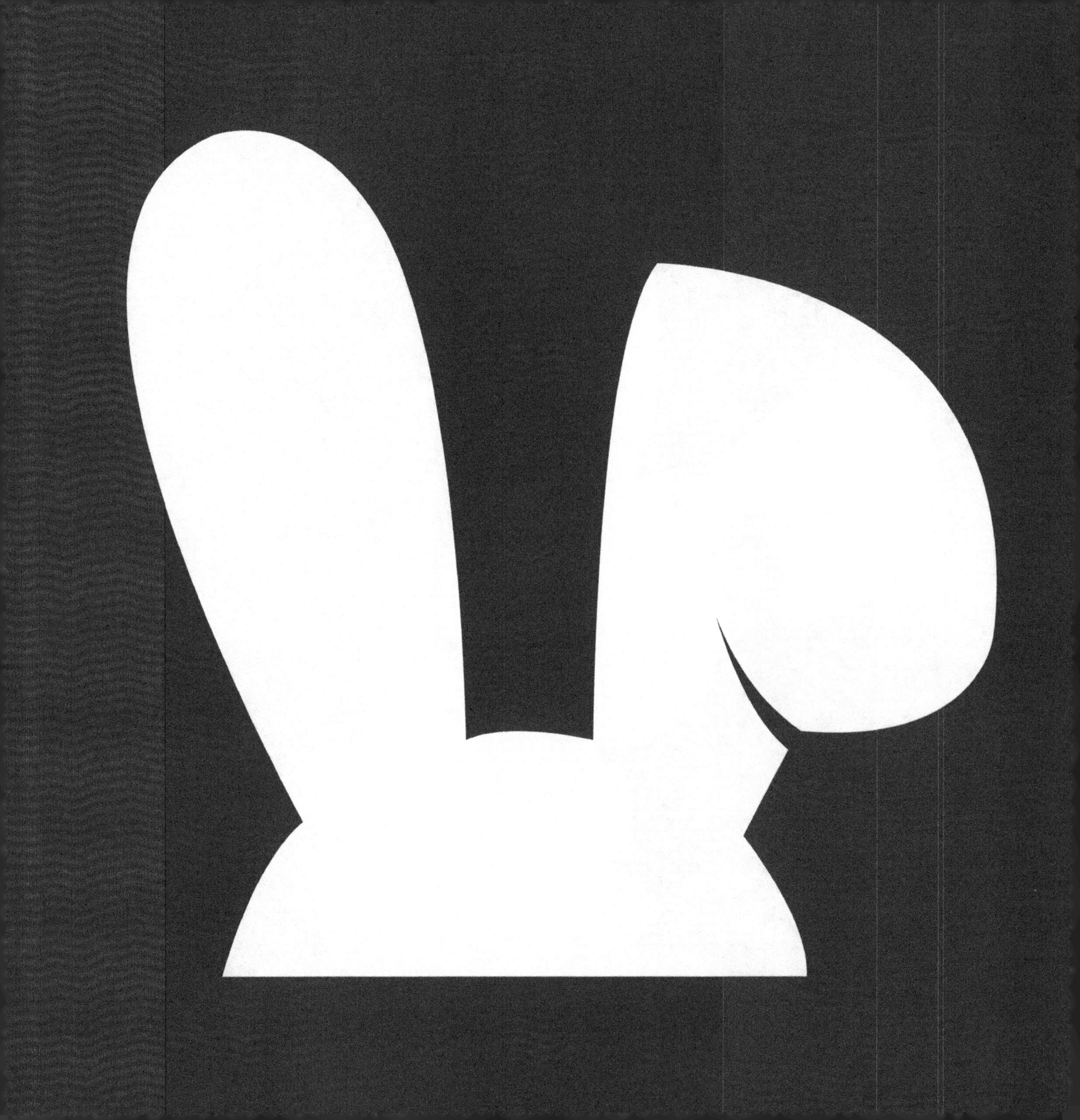

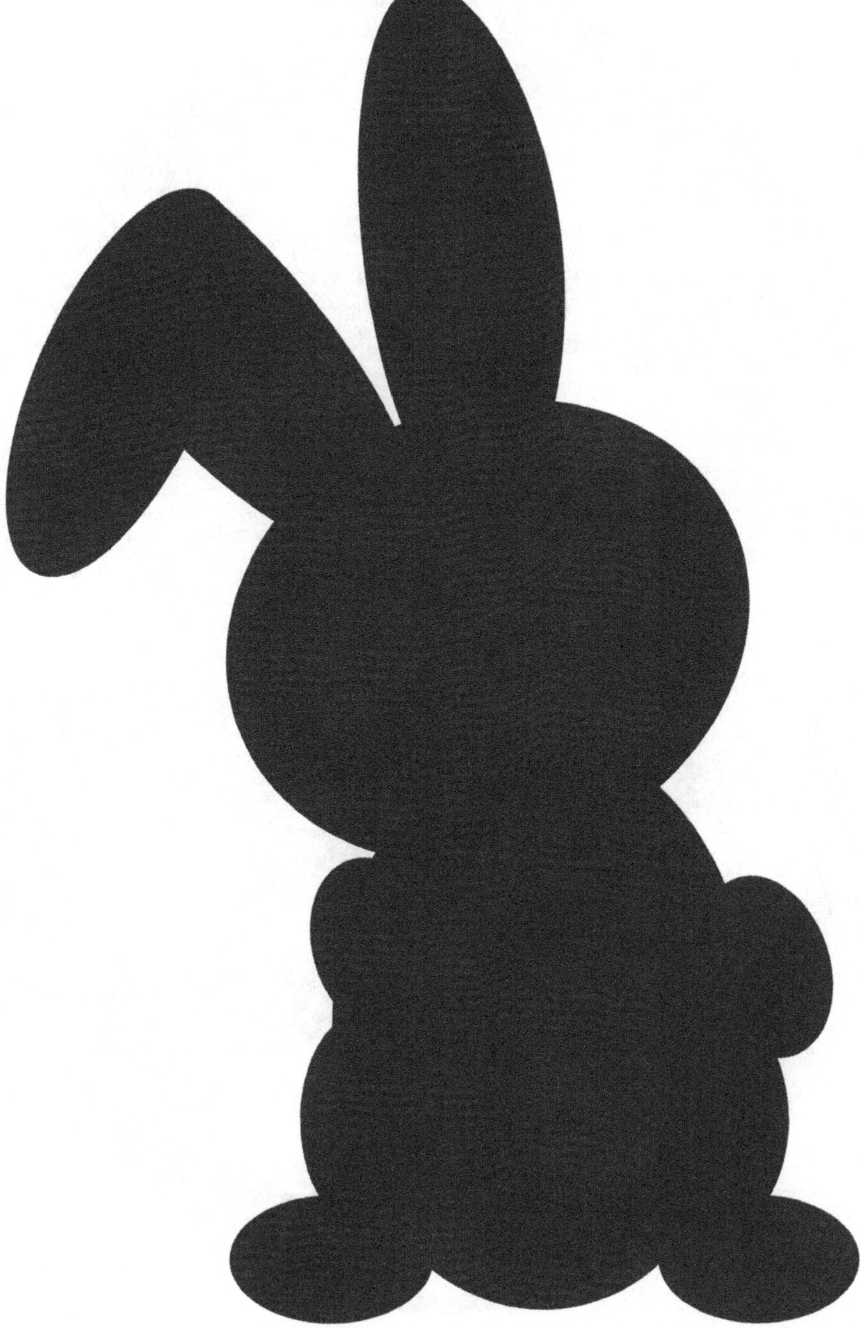

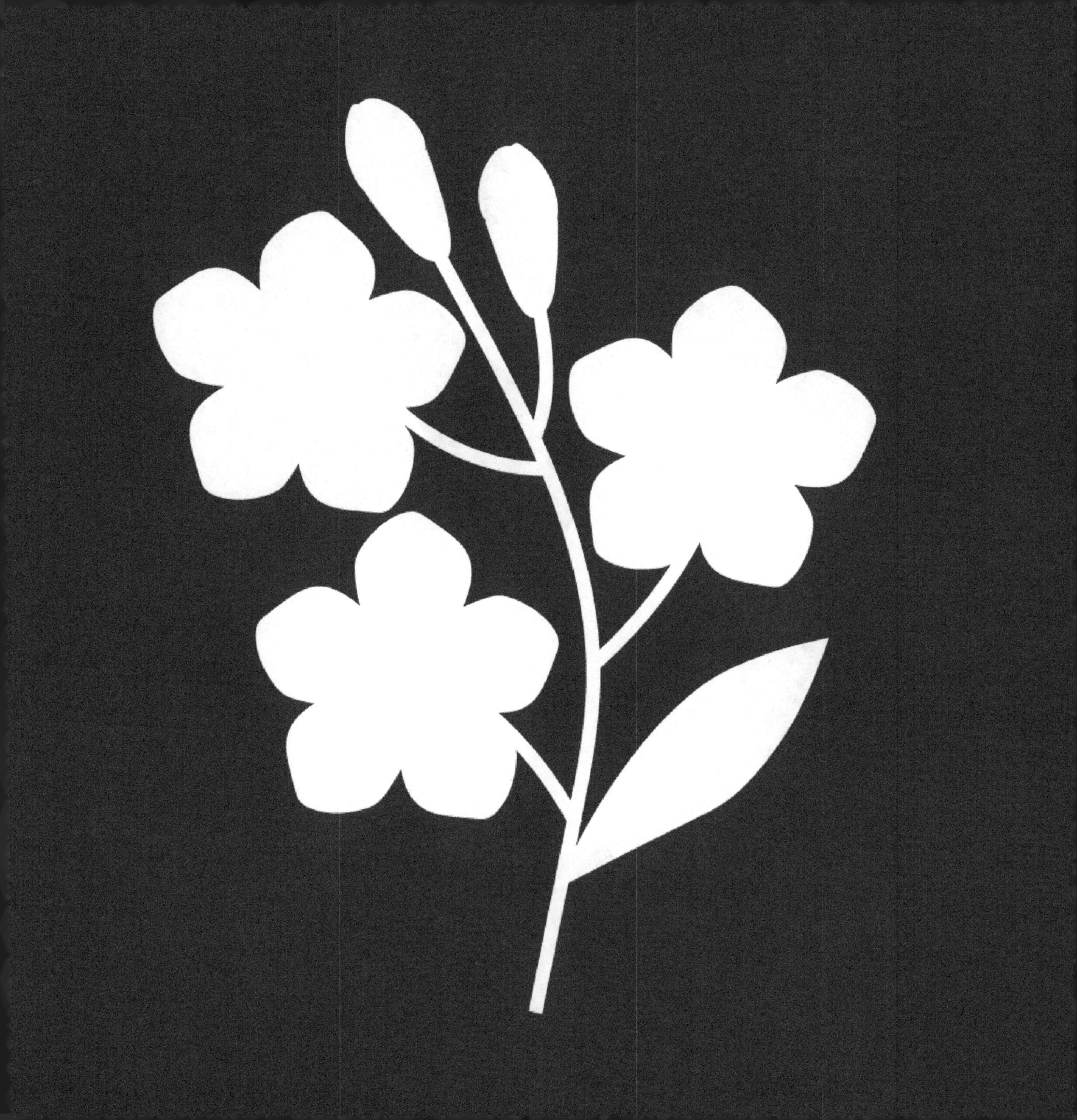

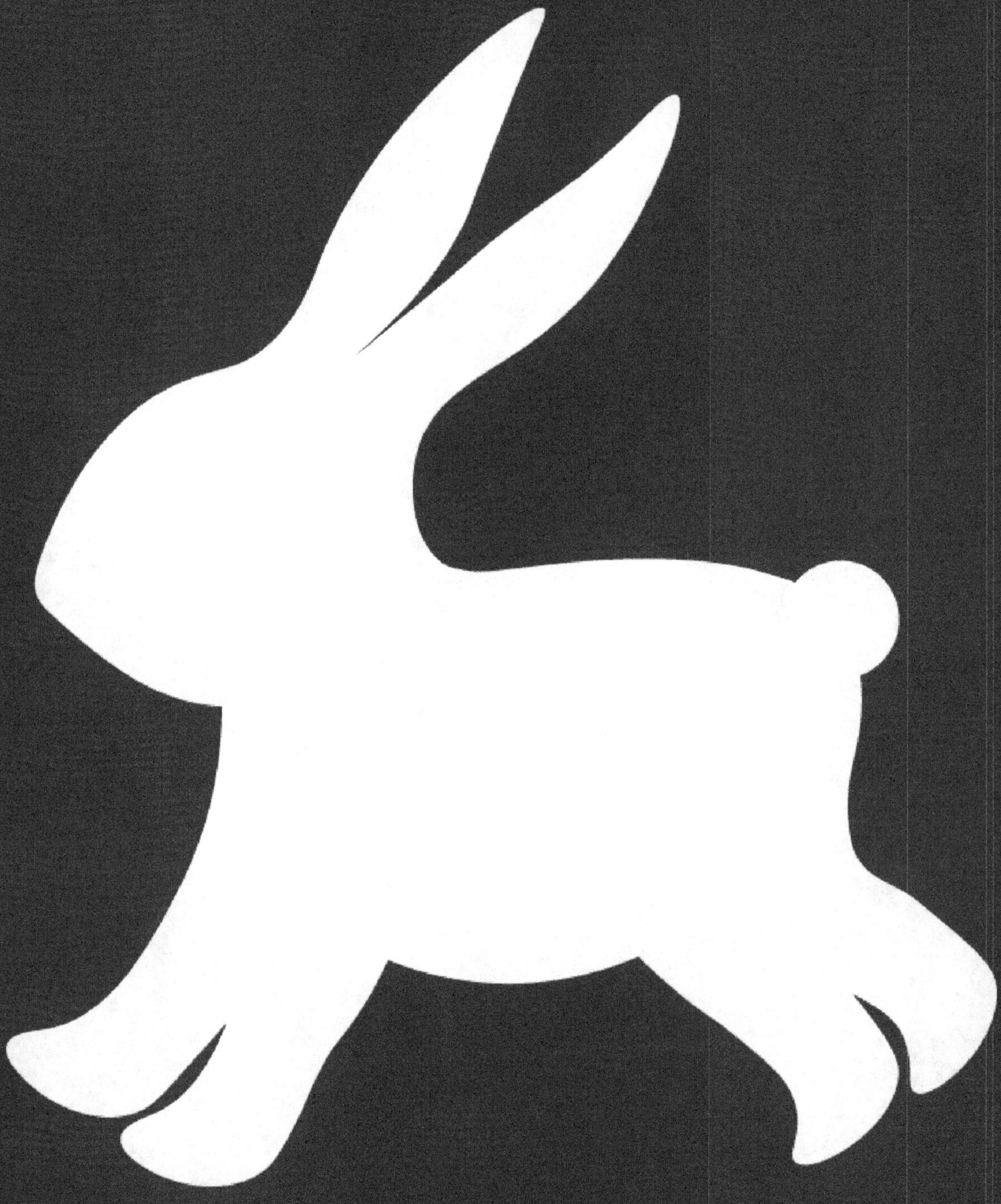

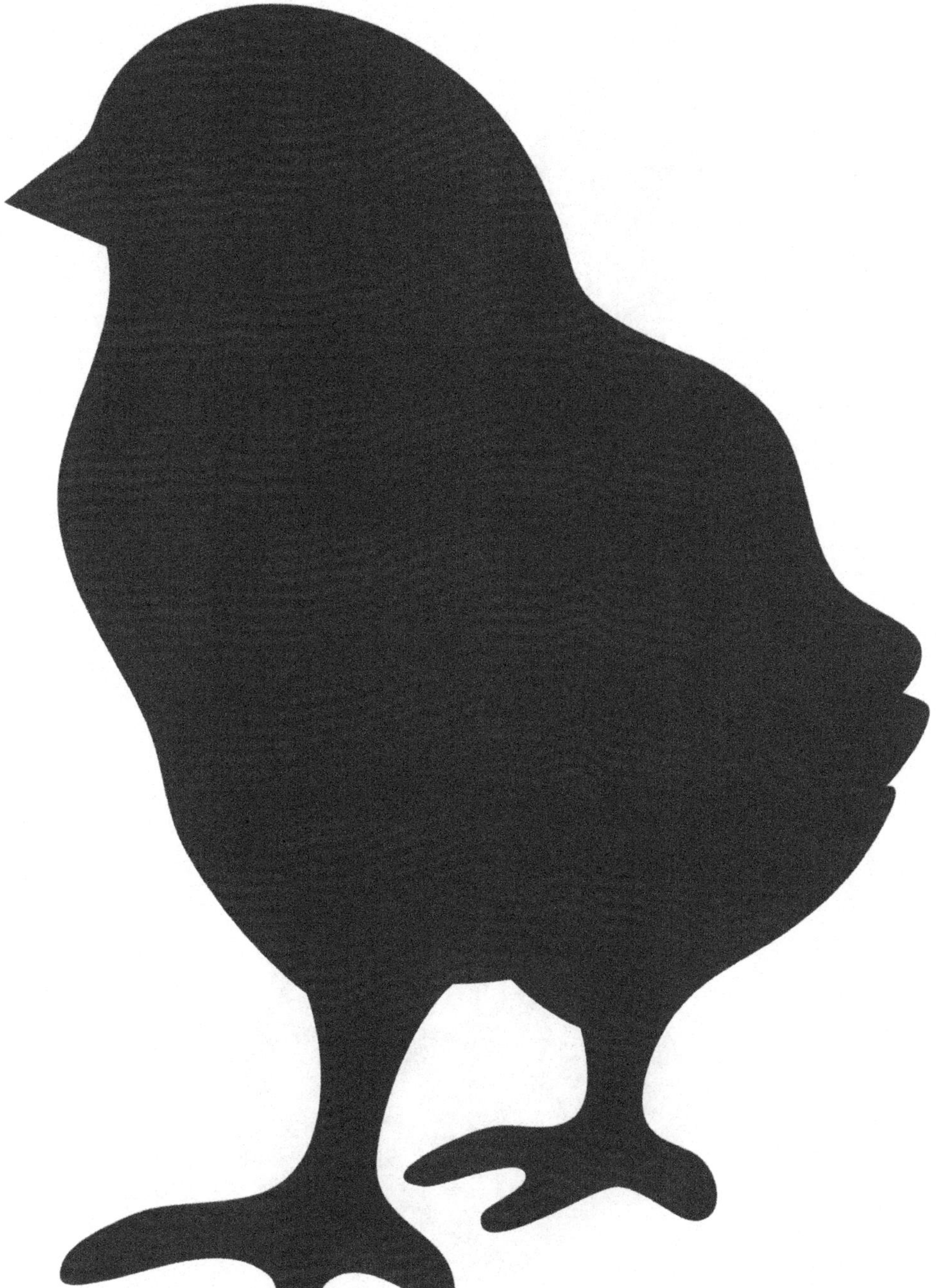

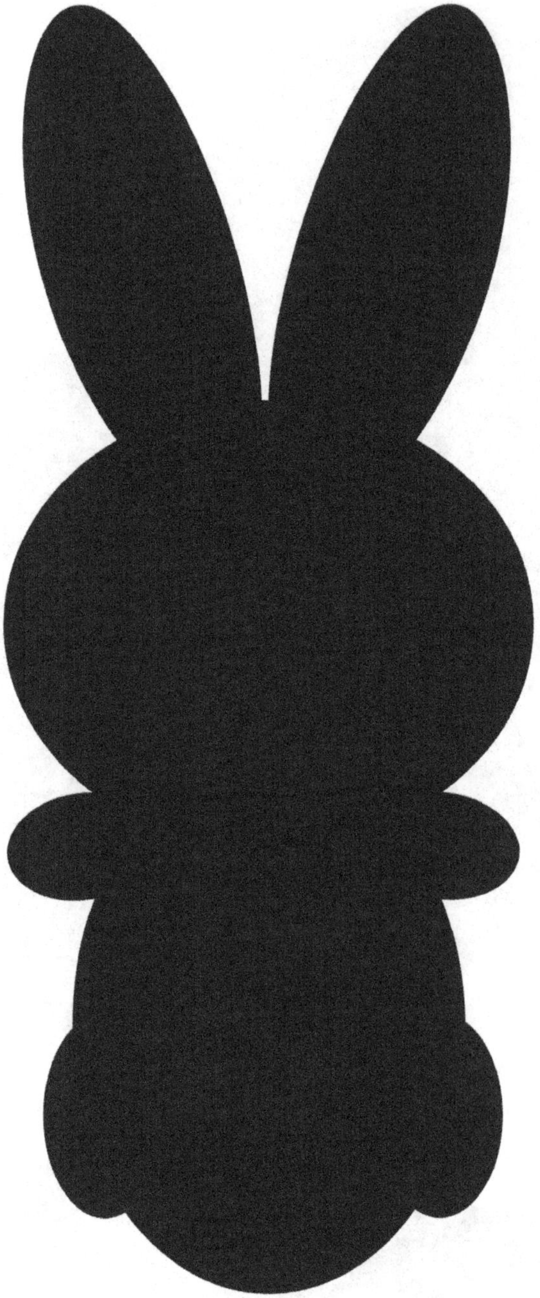

Made in the USA
Las Vegas, NV
02 March 2024

86594146R00057